Gay Fathers

Robert L. Barret
Bryan E. Robinson

Gay Fathers

Encouraging the Hearts of Gay Dads and Their Families

JOSSEY-BASS
A Wiley Company
San Francisco

Jossey-Bass books and products are available through most bookstores. To contact Jossey-Bass directly, call (888) 378-2537, fax to (800) 605-2665, or visit our website at www.josseybass.com.

Substantial discounts on bulk quantities of Jossey-Bass books are available to corporations, professional associations, and other organizations. For details and discount information, contact the special sales department at Jossey-Bass.

 Manufactured in the United States of America on Lyons Falls Turin Book. This paper is acid-free and 100 percent totally chlorine-free.

Library of Congress Cataloging-in-Publication Data

Barret, Robert L.
  Gay fathers : encouraging the hearts of gay dads and their families /
Robert L. Barret, Bryan E. Robinson. 1st [i.e. 2nd] ed.
    p. cm.
Originally published: Lexington, Mass. : Lexington Books, © 1990
Includes bibliographical references and index.
ISBN 0-7879-5075-0 (alk. paper)
1. Gay fathers—United States. 2. Gay fathers—Counseling of—United States.
I. Robinson, Bryan E. II. Title.
    HQ76.13 .B37
    306.874'2—dc21   00-032731

FIRST EDITION
HB Printing   10 9 8 7 6 5 4 3 2

Contents

100218

This book is dedicated to gay fathers, their children, wives, parents, brothers, and sisters who are developing alternative new families that affirm the rich potential of gay parenting.

Preface

In the ten years since *Gay Fathers* first appeared there has been a virtual revolution in the public's understanding of gay and lesbian people. Today it is not unusual to see gay characters on television or to read reports of the appointment of gay men and lesbians to important positions in both the public and private sectors. The decade of the 1990s surely will be remembered as a time when gay and lesbian people became more a part of mainstream America. Naturally this movement has faced considerable opposition, and one of the prime areas in which resistance continues to occur is that of gay parenting. Still, in urban areas across the country a "gayby boom" has quietly taken place. The privilege of parenting is no longer seen as an exclusive right of heterosexual persons. Gay men have begun to claim more assertively the right to parent. Men who have identified as gay from an early age are becoming fathers through adoption or surrogate mothers, or by serving as foster parents.

The first edition of this book played a role in that transformation. Initially sold primarily through gay bookstores to gay fathers who were looking for support in their efforts to be effective parents, the book became a resource for counselors, social workers, psychologists, and attorneys as well as others who wanted to know more about gay men who choose parenting. As the large chain bookstores began to include gay and lesbian titles, *Gay Fathers* began to reach a larger market.

Today gay fathers are not nearly as exotic as they were in 1990. School officials, clergy, social service professionals, and many in the general public have come to realize that gay and lesbian parents are effective in their roles and that their children do quite well. A continuing challenge is working with a legal system that seems unwilling to trust research findings about gay parenting. Unfortunately, in too many states, laws restrict the rights of gay fathers or do not allow them to openly adopt children.

Still, the number of married men who are coming out continues to grow, and those with children encounter the same questions they found in the past. What is the impact of gay fathering on child development? What hurdles can be anticipated and how might they be addressed? Do other gay fathers share my concerns? How do I come out to my children? What will my life be like if I live as a gay man? Parenting is no longer such a foreign topic in conversations between gay and lesbian people. Children of gay parents are showing up at social events, parades, churches, and schools. And there are more coming behind them. More students are coming in contact with gay parents and their children. The topic of gay parenting is not nearly as unusual in class discussions on child development as it used to be.

Back in 1990, almost as soon as we had sent the manuscript to the publisher, we had an urge to take it back and work on it more before publication. There had not been enough attention paid to men who become fathers through adoption or foster care. The law was changing rapidly, and we feared the book would be dated before it hit the bookshelves. The gay rights movement was taking major steps forward, and our sense was that gay fathering could become more of a focal point. We knew there would be more research published that would expand our knowledge about gay fathers.

Whereas Bryan Robinson and I collaborated equally on the first edition, he has not been available to assist with the revision. The revised edition contains work that both of us have done but that results from my vision and experience as a psychologist, a gay father, and gay grandfather. The book before you is different from the original in several ways. The literature, which continues to support the strengths of gay fathering, has been updated. New cases appear at the beginning of each chapter. There is more information on adoption and less information on HIV and AIDS. As a matter of fact, the chapter that had been devoted to AIDS has been dropped. In its place you will read about gay stepfathers, spiritual aspects of gay fathering, and gay grandparents. Our colleague, Claudia Flowers, whose area of expertise is research methodology, reviewed the gay fathering literature over the past decade and rewrote Chapter Seven. Finally, the original appendix of resources has been replaced by a listing of Internet resources. With so much information available electronically, it hardly seems necessary to use more paper and more space just to print lists of materials that are easily found using the Web.

There is much work that still needs to be done. As Dr. Flowers comments in Chapter Seven, the research findings are too impressionistic. There is a great need for well-designed research studies that generate knowledge about gay fathers. There are too many school counselors who do not know how to respond when a child, in the course of a session about grades or some other related matter, mentions that he or she has a gay father. There are too many children waiting to be adopted to justify denying a family experience to them solely because the potential adopters happen to be gay.

Working with gay fathers over the past twenty years has been a rare privilege. This past Easter I was asked to attend a party for gay fathers and their children. Watching those families play together was a wonderful experience. Today's children are growing up with a different understanding about what it means to be gay or lesbian. The day will come when gay families will be viewed just as other families. My hope is that this book will help us get closer to that goal.

ACKNOWLEDGMENTS

The list of names of those who have been instrumental in the revision of this book grows each day. The University of North Carolina at Charlotte has been generous in supporting our research. In particular, Dr. Mary Lynne Calhoun, chair of the Department of Counseling, Special Education and Child Development, has been steady in providing resources to support our work. Dean Jack Nagle and Vice Chancellor Denise Trauth have provided support in the form of a reassignment of duties that has allowed the senior author the time to complete this work. Further, the support of faculty colleagues and students has constantly encouraged us. And the special assistance of Ken Roess is gratefully acknowledged.

Gil Torre retyped the original manuscript, which no longer existed on disk. Claudia Flowers's work on Chapter Seven, as well as her willingness to read and make comments about the entire manuscript, has strengthened the book. The fathers who have volunteered their time either as research participants or as authors of case material have added to the depth of our knowledge about gay parents. Most of the fathers who wrote the cases that begin each chapter appear as themselves. In some instances, however, names and other identifying information have been altered to protect both the fathers and their children from public exposure. Without all these people, this book would not exist today.

May 2000   Bob Barret
Charlotte, North Carolina

Introduction and Overview

Carl and his partner, Wilson, live in a large city on the East Coast. Both of them have lived as self-identified gay men since their twenties and have been in a committed relationship for twelve years. They began six years ago to discuss the idea of parenting, and four years ago made arrangements to adopt their son. They are active parents and participate in many family activities along with other adoptive gay fathers.

For us, the question of having kids was one of those first big questions that arose when we recognized that our relationship was getting serious twelve years ago. As such, it was a make-or-break issue for our relationship. Neither of us wanted to take the relationship further if it wouldn't eventually include kids. From the moment that we had talked about it enough to realize that this was essential to our idea of a lifelong commitment, we began making all our decisions (about jobs, moves, finances, community involvement, and so on) with an eye on how they contributed to our creating a larger family.

We had good jobs and many longtime friends where we lived in Florida, but when a professional opportunity came along for one of us that would require that we move, we took it. Even though it meant leaving a new house that we had lived in for just barely a year, the move would also take us to a state where adoptions by gay dads are legal, unlike Florida. A lot of people, of all stripes, didn't understand why we would make such a radical change in our lives, but to us it was a way to get one step closer to our goal of parenthood. It really wasn't that big a sacrifice if you think of what our son went through, being abandoned and living in an orphanage before he came to live with us.

We talked about whether to adopt or to find a way of having biological kids. The more we talked about it, the more it made sense to adopt, especially since we were moving to a place where we could jointly adopt. There wouldn't be the issue of one of us having more claim to being "the" parent. Once we agreed that the surrogacy route wasn't right for us, then we had to decide about whether to adopt domestically or internationally. There had been lots of news about custody battles where gay and lesbian parents had lost fights with biological relatives of their kids. We decided to reduce that risk by adopting internationally. One of us had a problem with what felt like an issue of colonialism in doing this, but having to explain that concern someday to our kids seemed to pale in comparison to having to tell them why our family might be torn apart by a custody battle. Now that we're parenting a toddler, some of those more worldly, intellectual concerns seem less relevant—not less important, but less pressing.

When we had gotten settled into our new community and had figured out how we could make the adoption work with our careers (neither of us would work for the parental leave period, then one of us would only work part-time thereafter), we started examining all the different ways of adopting. We called an agency we heard of that worked well with gay and lesbian parents, but it was located too far from us, so they couldn't work with us. When we told the director our story, she was willing to spend an hour on the phone answering our questions about what we could and couldn't say to prospective agencies as we interviewed them. From this information we developed a script we would use to learn about an agency's willingness to work with a gay couple without having to identify ourselves as gay. It was strange having to do this, but one of the things we learned was that agencies had to protect their relationships with countries that did not allow queer folks to adopt. If we didn't tell the agency and it didn't ask, then the agency could portray us in the home study in a way that would be acceptable to the foreign country and leave the agency in a position of plausible deniability if it were asked about our sexual orientation at any point.

We interviewed about sixty agencies over the phone before we had a short list of those that we went to visit. Our first visit was with an agency that seemed fine over the phone, but when we got to the meeting, the director and program coordinator were clearly uncomfortable when they realized we were a gay couple. We left feeling very hurt and angry that they had given us a good liberal line over the phone but couldn't overcome their prejudice when we actually met. We went to other meetings that went much better and so winnowed our list down to two agencies that were highly recommended by parents who had been through their programs and that had good reports from the state agencies that license and oversee adoption agencies. The costs of their programs were comparable too. One was a large agency that didn't seem to have any gay or lesbian staff members (that we met at least), and the other was a small agency managed by out queer folks. What made the difference for us was that the small agency was quick to return our calls, was very thorough in answering our questions, and had a clear and logical explanation of the entire process; the other one just wasn't good about those things.

When we made our decision to start looking for an agency, we told our families what we were doing. Because we had been talking about this for years, they were generally enthusiastic. Some of them seemed to have some of the standard concerns for how others might tease our kids, so we had to spend some time helping them realize that the whole family could help our kids learn to deal with those kinds of problems and that in doing so we would become a stronger family. One of us had parents who were retiring about that time in another part of the country, and they decided to move to our city, in part to be closer to us. That has turned out to be a real blessing. Since our son's arrival, they have been an integral part of our lives and have given our son the gift of grandparenting at a really important time. We recognize how fortunate we are to enjoy this kind of support.

In moving to our new locale, we began to make friends with other gay and lesbian parents, other adoptive parents, and people from our professional lives. Since our son's arrival, our lives have come to include play dates and other social events focused on his social needs. Although generally this leaves much less time for the kind of interactions we used to have with our friends, most of those kinds of events that remain have evolved to be more kid friendly. We have come to be friends with a much wider and more enriching range of friends because of our becoming parents. It has also provided opportunities for nonqueer parents who have become friends to learn more about us, and many have remarked on the value of that learning to them.

One of the issues facing our immediate family is that none of us are of the same ethnicity. We have not had much direct conflict with racial bigotry, and although people may wonder why our son doesn't look like either of us, we suspect that there are enough mixed-race families in our area that we really don't stand out that much. So far, the biggest challenge has been to find adequate opportunities to expose our son to enclaves of people who share his ethnic background so that at least there are regular and frequent times when most everyone looks like him. As he grows and can offer his own opinions, we hope he will want to continue and even increase this kind of periodic immersion into his culture of birth, but if he chooses not to, we will respect his decisions.

Parenthood is a big change for us. The day-in, day-out responsibilities uplift and wear on us probably like they do on other parents. We may have some advantages though. By being adoptive parents, we have gone through a long and arduous journey to becoming parents, and that may have strengthened us to face some challenges just because we have already come over so many hurdles and withstood so many invitations not to proceed. It would have been easy for us not to be parents; what we went through to get here has made us stronger. By being queer parents, we have been coping with lots of new opportunities for growth for which our lives could not have prepared us. We both grew up in an American culture that taught people some little bit about being mixed-sex parents, and much of that doesn't apply for us. And what we learned about being gay men, and later a gay male couple, did not offer much in the ways of parenthood and the ways that being a parent affects our relationship and roles. By being queer adoptive parents, we have had to make up our roles and revisit our adaptations over and over again. Gay relationships are formed without the guide of gender-assigned roles, and each couple must face the demands of daily life, creating agreements about who will do what. Being queer has made the newness of such creations perhaps more familiar, and being adoptive parents in touch with lots of other adoptive parents may have made the strains of repeatedly changing roles more familiar, but nothing has made the experience of balancing all these factors predictable or nonthreatening as has the power of the love we feel from our son. It seems that his smile holds all the answers.

Carl and Wilson
Springfield, Massachusetts

In recent years gay, lesbian, bisexual, and transgendered (GLBT) citizens have been increasingly visible in demanding the basic rights guaranteed by the U.S. Constitution. As these men and women have marched, lobbied, and learned to use the media to tell their story, the American public has become more familiar with their issues and more supportive of their cause. We can see progress in the number of companies and governmental organizations that extend protection in terms of job security, if not full domestic partner benefits, to their sexual minority employees. Support groups for GLBT adolescents exist in most major cities. In the 1990s the gay community across the nation came out more fully, and it continues to successfully refute the long-held negative stereotypes of sexual minorities. It would appear that gay men and lesbians are poised to enter more fully into the mainstream of daily life. It is no longer so unusual for people to know a person who identifies as gay or lesbian. Even in the workplace, employee organizations of GLBT professionals are becoming almost commonplace. Once prevalent only in major metropolitan areas such as New York and San Francisco, gay and lesbian organizations are proliferating across the continent in virtually every metropolitan area. What appears to be a true change in social attitudes is clearly under way.

The gay parenting groups appearing in recent years are evidence of this new attitude. As gay men and lesbians throw off the negative attitudes that have limited their freedom, it is becoming increasingly common to see and hear them discussing parenting issues. Such questions as Should we have children? Where do we go to find an adoption agency that is open to sexual minorities? What about becoming foster parents? are common, as gay men and lesbians form relationships that closely parallel those created by heterosexual couples. In a survey of gay couples, one-third of the respondents under age thirty-five indicated they are considering becoming parents (Bryant & Demian, 1994). More and more gay men and lesbians are finding a rich source of life satisfaction in parenting.

The idea of two men becoming parents was once considered radical and even was seen by some gay activists as a sellout to heterosexism. Becoming involved with a gay man who had children was often seen as a betrayal of the gay rights movement. "Real gay men don't need to mimic the lives of straights by buying into the foundations of their lifestyle," said some leaders. Men shied away from involvement with children, fearing they might be accused of sexual molestation, an attribute of the negative image of gay men promoted by conservative groups. Still, the gay fathering movement has grown, and as many young gay men explore their expanding options, they too can dream of sharing their lives with children. The good news is that research consistently shows that they have the ability to be successful parents (Patterson, 1992) and that their influence on their children is like that of all parents.

A particular problem in learning about gay fathers is the nature of research studies (Patterson, 1994). Although the professional literature has addressed this question for more than twenty-five years (Bell & Weinberg, 1978), the number of studies is small, and firm conclusions are difficult to make (Patterson & Chan, 1996). This means that throughout this book, references will be made to studies that may not reflect more contemporary realities. This problem is apparent when one attempts to determine the population percentage of sexual minorities. The Kinsey studies (Kinsey, Pomeroy, & Martin, 1948) suggested that 10 percent of men in the United States were homosexual, and that figure was considered the reference point for years. Determining the number of a population that has largely been closeted is a very complex and often unscientific task, and most recent research places the number of gay men at 5 percent (Gagnon, Laumann, Michael, & Michaels, 1994). Determining the number of gay men who are fathers is equally complex. Spada (1979) estimates that 20 percent of gay men have been married, whereas Miller (1979a) suggests that between 20 and 50 percent of these men have been married. It is likely that the number of children fathered by gay men is between two and four million (Patterson & Chan, 1996). Whatever the figure may be, the emergence of gay men and lesbians who are parents can be seen in a growing body of professional and popular literature.

Gay fathers have also become more visible as part of the new attention that has been devoted to fathering in general. Before the 1970s, a single father's having custody of his children was viewed as unusual and in violation of the "best interest of the child" doctrine. In the United States, the number of custodial single fathers has grown from 1.7 million in 1995 to 2.7 million in 1998, an increase of 59 percent (Barts, 1999). This increase is due to courts understanding more fully that men can function quite well as primary parents to their children. Fortunately, today we now know that fathers make good "mothers" too, and virtually all elements of society have come to acknowledge the unique role that fathering plays in child development (Lamb, 1986).

It is certainly true that our communities are becoming more comfortable with the idea of gay parenting, but there are still serious obstacles facing those gay men who want to live openly with their children. The purpose of this chapter is to provide an overview of the legal and psychological challenges facing gay fathers. Understanding that gay fathers, like all parents, constitute a diverse group is a fundamental first step in refuting the negative stereotype that depicts gay men as unfit to be parents.

PATHWAYS TO PARENTHOOD

Gay men become parents through various processes. Most have their children while living heterosexual lives that include marriage to women (Green & Bozett, 1991). Others find themselves parenting by becoming foster parents or through adoption. Some even arrange to have children by coparenting with lesbian women or through surrogate mothers who have been inseminated with an egg fertilized by their sperm. We know the most about the formerly married gay men who have children, because they frequently appear in court hearings involving issues of child custody (Patterson, 1992). But in large metropolitan areas across the country, men like Carl and Wilson, who have identified as gay all of their adult lives, are taking steps to become fathers, and it is simply a matter of time before researchers will begin telling us about them. One of these men, Billy, told us, "I had always wanted to be a father, and I really couldn't see why it wouldn't work. Jim and I had been together for twelve years. We mixed our sperm together, and a friend of ours was artificially inseminated. We're not sure who Tom's 'real' father is. What's important is that both of us love him and are proud to claim him as a son. He seems to like the idea of having two daddies as well as a mommy."

The reasons that gay men choose to become parents are every bit as diverse as those of heterosexual men (Robinson & Barret, 1986). These men become parents and strive to create lives that offer security and happiness for their children as well as themselves. It is important to validate the very strong contributions that gay men can make in their fathering roles (Shordone, 1993). Whether with the assistance of a mental health professional or on their own, gay fathers must juggle a number of very complex issues as they integrate their life roles.

There is no one model of parenting style that can be seen among all gay fathers. Each gay father lives in a unique environment. He may have total or no family support. He may have a boyfriend or partner or may not date at all. He may be out to everyone in his life or might cling tenaciously to the safety of his closet. Some men live in communities where the school system has become sensitized to the unique needs of gay families. Others fear that coming out to their children's teachers might lead to negative attitudes that the child would have to face.

The bottom line is that gay fathers fit no one mold; people who interact with them need to suspend a tendency to view them as a class. Although there are many things gay fathers have in common, the ways they manage their lives are very individual. One thing they share is that they are raising their children in social environments that typically are not supportive of gay relationships; thus they must prepare their children to live in communities that may express negative attitudes about their fathers. Another is that they worry about the legal system insofar as it may deny them access to their children.

LEGAL ISSUES

Although research has shown that a father's homosexuality has little impact on the development of his children's identity, courts are reluctant to place children in a gay father's care. The legal system has enforced a double standard whereby heterosexual couples are presumed to manage the expression of their sexuality in appropriate ways, but gay fathers are assumed to flaunt their sexuality before their innocent children (Walters & Elam, 1985). In general, we cannot rely on the court system to have a complete understanding of gay parenting. One psychologist told us,

> I was serving as an expert witness in a child custody hearing. The judge became frustrated because she had been unable to find any information about gay parents. Fortunately the local Children's Law Center understood that being gay did not automatically disqualify a man from being an effective parent. Still, the mother of the children, represented by an attorney supplied by a conservative religious group, prevailed, and the children were awarded to her. Three years later, three of those four boys are living with their father with the court's consent. The change in custody was secured only after many had helped this judge find research studies on gay parenting, and the boys had reached an age where they were better able to make their own choices.

Many gay men have used the courts to gain their rights to active parenting, and fortunately the courts appear to be gaining a better understanding that gay men can serve in the role of parents. As recently as 1991, a review of custody decisions revealed that the courts continue to favor the mother (Rivera, 1991). However, in some cases, the courts reluctantly awarded custody to fathers because it was clear that the mother was unfit. Some judges must choose between two suitable parents, and more and more frequently, particularly when the mother has been shown to be an ineffective parent, they will either award sole or joint custody to gay men. In some of these cases homosexual teenagers who have either run away from or been abandoned by their families have been placed with gay foster parents who are able to provide positive models of gay relationships (Harry, 1983).

Most state courts, however, continue to base their decisions on myths and negative stereotypes. Their views are augmented by the claims of more conservative groups who see the gay rights movement as antifamily. For example, in 1990, voters in San Francisco were asked to enact a domestic partner law that would enable gay men and lesbians to extend their employee benefits to their partners, including them on health insurance plans and providing emergency or sick leave when the partner was ill. Assailed by conservative religious groups as a direct threat to the family, the law was defeated. By 1998, however, that law had been passed, and the San Francisco board of supervisors (city council) even refused to do business with companies that did not have similar policies. By the beginning of the millennium, United, Delta, US Airways, and other leading corporations began to offer employees domestic partner benefits.

The recommendations of social workers, juvenile parole officers, psychiatrists, psychologists, and other professionals who harbor negative attitudes about homosexuals frequently bolster the "antifamily" bias. Homophobia, or fear of homosexuals, is a deeply ingrained and often subtle attitude that undermines our ability to see gay men and lesbians as the human beings they are. It has been suggested that such attitudes are really more reflective of a *hatred* of homosexuals, or homoprejudice (Logan, 1996), that will change only through a direct, aggressive, positive public relations campaign carefully designed to allay the public's fears of gay men and lesbians (Kirk & Madsen, 1989).

In the meantime, courts continue to make decisions in support of a model of the traditional family that may no longer exist. As recently as 1990, the court's denial of homosexual parents' contact with their children was frequently based on the "immoral and unacceptable" character of homosexuals. A particular problem is that in many states, sexual intercourse between two men is still against the law, and courts find themselves in a bind when awarding custody of a minor to a father who openly lives with another man. This issue is often addressed when courts award custody but admonish gay fathers not to include their children in a gay lifestyle.

Kirk Smith had been a successful father of two sons who lived with him since their births. In 1991 his ex-wife left the two boys with him when she moved to Kansas to live with her lover, whom she later married. In 1995 Smith's ex-wife sued for sole custody on the basis that the two boys, ages twelve and nine, were suffering as a result of living with their father and his partner, Tim Tipton. In overturning the appeals court decision, the North Carolina Supreme Court pointed out that Smith and Tipton kissed each other in the presence of the boys and that, although they kept the door locked when having sex, they let the children come into the bedroom when they were still in bed together. The lone dissenting justice, John Webb, stated, "There is virtually no evidence showing that these acts by the defendant have adversely affected the two children. The test should be how the action affects the children and not whether we approve of it. . . . I do not believe that we should allow a change of custody on evidence which shows only that the defendant is a practicing homosexual" (Lambda Legal Defense and Education Fund, 1998). Subsequent court rulings in North Carolina have supported this case and have led many gay fathers to carefully monitor their relationships and even to avoid setting up joint housekeeping with their partners. Mike Godley, a gay attorney who represents many gay fathers, told us, "This ruling just about cuts out gay fathers from having live-in relationships if they hope to have joint or sole custody of their children. And I am beginning see some cases where overnight visitation may be denied because of the presence of a partner in the gay father's home. The ruling does apply to both gay and straight couples, but the straight couples who are not married do have the choice of making their relationship legal. Gay men don't have that option." Similar court rulings have been handed down in New Jersey and Maryland. Most gay fathers continue to have their children overnight less than their ex-wives (Stradler, 1993), and some courts only allow daytime visits (Campbell, 1994). Some gay fathers are learning that in order to act as fathers, they must once again slip back into the oppression of a closeted lifestyle. The loneliness they report as they watch the gay community becoming ever more visible can turn into a bitterness that may have a negative influence on the children.

Changes do seem to be coming. In Massachusetts, New York, and California, public policy forbids discrimination based on affectional or sexual orientation in foster care and custody decisions. And recent favorable court decisions affirming the rights of gay men and lesbians to adopt children are creating legal precedents that may have significant impact across the country (Herscher, 1989). Attorneys from the Lambda Legal Defense and Education Fund report a trend away from denying custody solely on the basis of the father's sexual orientation (Lambda Legal Defense and Education Fund, 1997). Rather than rely on sexual orientation *per se* as a reason to deny custody, the courts are more and more frequently focusing on the child's best interest. This "nexus" (clear connection) approach means that there must be evidence showing that the parents' sexual orientation is damaging to the children. As recently as 1995, twenty-nine states had adopted some version of a nexus test.

While this kind of progress is being made, challenges continue largely from the political influence of the religious right. Gay men who seek fatherhood through adoption need to be prepared to go to court to guarantee their rights (Ricks, 1995). New Hampshire and Florida are the only states where gay men have been barred from the adoption process, but similar laws are under consideration in other state legislatures. In 1998, the District of Columbia adopted a policy that denies gay men and lesbians the right to adopt children. Once passed, these laws are challenged in the courts by gay men, sometimes with the support of social services agencies, who want to provide secure family lives for children who otherwise would remain in the foster child system. In New York, an appellate court overturned the family court's ruling that denied a gay man from adopting the two children who had flourished under his care while he was a foster parent. This ruling found that single status was not sufficient to deny adoption (Lambda Legal Defense and Education Fund, 1997).

Most foreign countries do not allow single males to adopt, although international adoptions are a commonplace avenue for gay fathers. Finding children in other countries is complex and requires the use of a reputable adoption agency. Remember how Carl and Wilson identified sixty agencies before selecting one that would work with them? Arranging adoption in both European and Asian countries is one way to circumvent local laws that prevent gay men from adopting. Foreign adoption is not without significant risks, however. One gay father told us he had arranged an adoption in a South American country, went to get his daughter, and ended up having to stay in the country for over seven months while legal documents moved through a system that was not at all concerned about his need to return to work. Rather than return home, he chose to stay put to monitor the situation. While waiting, he was able to gain insight into his daughter's culture and brought her home only after the two of them had developed a very strong relationship, sparing her from having to adjust to a new home and a new family at the same time. Gay men considering foreign adoption must carefully analyze legal systems that may differ very much from our own.

Currently the choice is restricted to China, Cambodia, Vietnam, and Moldavia. Although these countries do allow *single men* to adopt, it is likely they would balk at the idea of two *gay men* having one of their children. To adopt internationally, one partner in the couple becomes the applicant, and once that adoption has been completed and the child is in the home, the other partner applies for adoption under the laws of the state in which they reside.

Another legal issue for many gay couples is second-parent adoption. Until very recently, only one member of a gay couple could adopt. By 1997, second-parent adoptions by gay and lesbian couples had become legal in the District of Columbia (refuted in 1998) and twenty-one states (Lambda Legal Defense and Education Fund, 1997). Joint adoption offers a substantial support to gay couples and encourages them to work out their differences rather than to separate prematurely when discouraged about the future of the relationship. Recall that Carl and Wilson moved, in part, because their new home state allowed second-parent adoption.

Some gay men seek out lesbian couples with whom they coparent, and others find women who agree to serve as surrogate mothers (Patterson & Chan, 1996). These processes involve complex legal arrangements that the court may void if custody is challenged. Gay men choosing this path must consult with an attorney skilled in the legalities of gay parenting. Costs can range up to $60,000 when surrogate mothers are involved. Bernie, who became a father this way, told us, "I have known all along that I wanted to be a father. With the help of an attorney, I found a woman who donated an egg that was inseminated with my sperm and then implanted in another woman's uterus. The surrogate mother is five months pregnant now, and I expect to be present when my son is born. Both women have signed documents giving sole custody to me. I worry that one might change her mind, and then I will experience even higher legal costs. I know I will be a good father and can't wait to get started."

Whatever the means by which gay men become fathers, one fundamental awareness is that the research is consistent in showing that they and their children can flourish in this nontraditional family (Patterson, 1992). As more research studies on gay parenting appear and as more courts rely on a nexus approach, we can expect that access to parenting by gay men and lesbians will become more common. And as judges set aside their prejudices, they too will be able to see that being gay does not automatically disqualify men and women from being effective parents. Undertaking a costly and emotionally draining court battle is not a project taken on whimsically.

Those gay men and lesbians who brave such an undertaking are slowly changing a system that has all too often been indifferent to gay rights.

CHALLENGES FACING GAY FATHERS

Being a successful parent is not easy for any father, but being a successful gay father is even more difficult. Gay men can be victimized by both heterosexual and homosexual worlds and often by their families, former spouses, and children. Heterosexuals generally consider homosexual fathers to be strange. Some think the terms *gay* and *father* are mutually exclusive, failing to understand why a homosexual man would marry or want to be a parent. Gay fathers are accused of marrying and parenting only to hide their homosexuality, although such accusations are not generally borne out by personal accounts or research findings. As we discuss later, heterosexual society suspects gay fathers of child molestation, causing blurred sexual identity in their children, providing a poor home environment, and subjecting their children to stigmatization (Marciano, 1985).

Gay fathers are a minority within a minority. Whereas children provide increased status in the heterosexual world, they often are a stigma not easily accepted by homosexuals (Bozett, 1984b). As Dennis told us after he had met a father with three sons, "No thanks. I don't want to get involved with him. My life is complicated enough. I surely can't compete with that." The homosexual single world does not easily accept "diaper talk," PTA meetings, and early departures from social events to relieve the baby-sitter (Fadiman, 1983). The singles-oriented homosexual community is not used to children; some gay men find they prefer not to have children around and resent their interference with independence unless the child is emancipated or the gay father abrogates his parental responsibilities. They find it difficult to cope with how completely children can captivate a parent (Maddox, 1982). Children are also proof of heterosexual activity, and some gay men find that unacceptable. The gay partner may also resent the child, or there may be competition between partner and child, as one father told us:

> Both Hunter and my son became jealous of my attention. I felt torn between the two; each demanded more of my time than I was able to give. This was an irritant in my relationship with Hunter, a relationship that already lacked focus. Four months into the school year, our relationship had almost completely broken down. We still occupied the same apartment, but our love for each other, which we had openly shared with my son, had turned into hostility. My son perceived this hostility and became protective of me, and I felt defensive of his habits, which I knew bothered Hunter.

Gay fathers who are married struggle with having a divided identity. As the need to express their homosexuality becomes stronger over time, marriages are sure to run into difficulties. Wives often do not know of the husband's homosexuality, particularly because many of the husbands only gradually become aware of their homosexuality after marriage. Some couples stay together "for the sake of the children," perhaps giving the husband one night "out with the boys," or the husband may try to suppress his homosexuality. Others divorce or separate, which typically leads to disputes about the children and what role the gay father and his partner will play in the lives of the children (Gochros, 1989).

A challenge for formerly married gay fathers is to reconcile the duality of having identified as heterosexual and now identifying as homosexual. What is gained in one world usually results in losses in the other. Inability to satisfy two standards of behavior results in alienation, loss of self-esteem, helplessness, and frustration. It is apparent that gay fathers must learn to cope with rejection and isolation from both homosexual and heterosexual worlds. As marginal beings, gay fathers can become extremely frustrated trying to find a place to fit in. Social scientists recognize that gay fathers are victims of both homosexual and heterosexual worlds because they have two identities that are at opposite extremes of social acceptance (Bozett, 1983). Research suggests that gay fathers must resolve the disparity between their homosexual feelings and heterosexual behaviors. Gay fathers live in what has been dubbed a double closet. They leave the first closet when they disclose their homosexuality, the second when they reveal their fatherhood to other homosexuals (Bozett, 1984b; Fadiman, 1983).

Even dating can become complicated for gay fathers. Roger, a young gay man, spoke about his reluctance to get involved with one father:

> I suddenly find myself living in the suburbs, driving his kids to school, ball games, and McDonald's. I miss the easy freedom of city life and often find myself resenting the fact that his kids control my life as well as his. It helped when I started spending time in the city with friends on one of the weekend nights he has his kids. That way, they have private time together, and I can get away and enjoy myself. I'm not sure how long this can last, but for now it works because I love him and would rather be with him, even in the suburbs and with his kids.

Interviews indicate that many once-married gay fathers had been satisfied with their marriages, and the majority of these men (65.6 percent) considered the basic problem in their marriages to be the emergence of their homosexuality, not incompatibility (Wyers, 1987). The impact of divorce and separation was more devastating to these men's wives than to the men themselves, although divorced gay fathers experienced a range of emotions from excitement and relief to identity confusion, guilt, depression, and loss.

Such a transition generates significant personal change. Brian Miller (1978) reported that the thirty gay husbands he interviewed went through an adolescent-like sexual reawakening and resocialization as they began to affirm their new sexual identity:

> Homosexually oriented husbands tend to move from
> covert highly compartmentalized lifestyles, with all the

surface appearances of suburban matrimonial accommo-
dation, toward open, often militant, gay stances. Although ruptured marriages are left in the wake of this
movement, these men consistently maintain commitment to and responsibility for their children, insofar as
the courts allow. Such resocialization and consequent adjustments to life in a differing cultural milieu are seen as
resulting not only from a complex process of negotiating, in which cognitive dissonance is resolved, but also
from the initiation of a homosexual love relationship.
The latter appears stronger than any other factor in enabling the husband to reassess the potentialities of gay
lifestyles and identities [p. 229].

Miller (1979b) also found that when gay men leave their spouses
and acquire a homosexual lifestyle, they experience enhanced self-
esteem and a disappearance of psychosomatic ailments (such as
headaches, ulcers, and fatigue). Our case reports support these findings indicating the father's emotional relief from having to restrain
his true self. Stories like that of Chip can allay gay fathers' fears of
rejection by their children. As anxiety is reduced, feelings of self-
esteem and security are enhanced.

Children Living on the Fringe

My name is Chip, and I'm seventeen and in twelfth grade. When we
first moved to Indianapolis, I learned my dad was gay; I was twelve.
I didn't really think much about it. There was a birthday coming up,
and Dad said we were going to go out and buy a birthday card. He
went out, drove around the block, and then parked back in front of
our house. Then he took me to the park and told me the facts of life.
He asked me if I knew what it meant to be gay. I told him, "Yeah, it
means to be happy and enjoy yourself." Then he started to explain

to me about being homosexual. I really didn't know what it was at that point, until he explained it to me.

It's an accepted part of my life now. I've been growing up with it for almost ten years. When he invites another guy into the house, it's OK. I don't bring other kids home. One of my friends is extremely homophobic, and he lets that fact be known. I wouldn't dare risk anything, or it would be like "good-bye" to my friend. My other two friends, I don't know how they would react. So I have to be careful about having certain friends over. To me it's blatantly obvious. Having been exposed to so many gay people, I know what to look for and what I'm seeing. Sometimes it's kind of hard because people make fun of gay people. And if I stick up for their rights, then I get ridiculed. So I just don't say anything at school. It's kind of hard sometimes.

The good thing is that you get more of an objective view of people in general, being raised by someone who's so persecuted by society. You begin to sympathize with anyone who is persecuted by society. You tend not to be as prejudiced. You tend to appreciate people for what they are, just personally, as opposed to color, religion, or sexual preference. That's the best thing. The hardest thing is hearing all these people making cracks or jokes on TV or at school and not really being able to do anything about it. Because he's my dad after all. It makes me kind of sad. I never feel ashamed or embarrassed, but I do feel a little pressured because of this. One time a friend of mine made a joke about gay people. I just played it off like I thought it was funny, but I didn't. You have to pretend that you think the same thing they do when you don't. That makes me feel like a fraud.

When my dad puts his arm around another man, the first thing I think is, I could never do that. It makes me a little bit uncomfortable, but I'm not repulsed by it. There are times I wish he wouldn't do it. When he first came out to me, the only question I asked him was, "What are the chances of me being gay?" He couldn't answer it. But today, to the best of my knowledge, I'm not gay. I like chasing after girls.

Sometimes I feel like I'm keeping a big secret. My dad had a holy union with a man once. My friends had these big plans, and we were all going out on the day of this big event. And I couldn't go and couldn't explain why. Things like that have happened a number of times. I can't go, and I can't tell why. They start yelling at me and get mad. They'll get over it; it's none of their business.

As fathers go, mine tends to be a little nicer—almost a mother's temperament. A friend of mine's father is strict and almost never acknowledges that my friend's even there. Another friend's father doesn't spend much time with him. They just seem to have stricter parents than mine. I don't know if that's just because of my dad's personality in general or if it's because he's gay. He's a very emotional person; he cries easily. I love him. He's a good dad. He's more open than other dads. He doesn't let me get away with a lot. He tends to be more worried about me and a girl together than some other fathers are about their sons—more worried about my having sex. Whenever I go out on a date, he always says something like, "Don't do anything I wouldn't do," only he doesn't say it jokingly. Sometimes he's just overly cautious.

If I could change my dad and make him straight, I wouldn't do it. It might make things easier for me in some ways, but I wouldn't have grown up the way I have. Being exposed to the straight world and gay world equally has balanced me out more than some of the other people I know. The only thing I'd want to change is society's treatment of him.

GAY MEN IN THERAPY: AN OVERVIEW

The history of gay men as consumers of psychotherapy is not altogether positive. Experiencing rejection in their personal lives, many gay men also encounter a counselor who has not resolved his or her own homophobic attitudes. As part of his coming out, Bill consulted with four different therapists before he found one who would take his homosexuality seriously:

> The first three listened to me for a bit and then said something like, "Oh, Bill, you're not homosexual." Naturally, I was relieved to hear that, but in each instance the sexual attraction to men did not go away! So it took me twenty years to finally decide that I was going to get some help with this issue. I realized that the men and women I had approached for help were dealing with their own discomfort about homosexuality and were unable to really hear my issues. Now I am seeing someone who has been quite helpful. He keeps insisting that I am not gay but probably bisexual, and he thought I made a big mistake when I told my kids, but he's the best I can find in this community. I finally told him that if he could not stop telling me I am bisexual I would just terminate the therapy. That pretty much shut him up, but I still worry about his judging me. It's too bad there are not more openly gay therapists here. That's what I really need.

Bill's situation is not unusual outside of major metropolitan areas. In spite of the fact that an estimated 25 to 65 percent of gay men seek mental health services (a rate two to four times higher than for heterosexuals), satisfaction is low (Bell & Weinberg, 1978; Jay & Young, 1979; Rudolph, 1988). To a certain extent Bill's experience points out the role that homophobia plays for both individuals in the counseling relationship. Perhaps one reason Bill waited so long to come to terms with his sexuality was that he was simply too afraid to face that aspect of himself to present it to a counselor in stronger and more determined terms; it is also possible that a more gay-positive counselor might have helped Bill address these issues much earlier.

In 1973, the American Psychiatric Association (APA) formally redefined homosexuality, removing it from a list of pathologies and stating that it implied "no impairment in judgement, stability, or general social or vocational capabilities" (American Psychiatric Association, 1974, p. 497). Although rejected by over one-third of APA members, this ruling effectively ended the labeling of homosexuality as a diagnosable mental illness. However, research studies continue to indicate that the rank and file of psychiatry still hold negative views of homosexuals.

Isay (1989) presents the most compelling review of the impact of the APA's change of definition on psychiatry and concludes that the profession still has a long way to go in ridding itself of a damaging homophobia. Rudolph (1988, p. 167) concludes his review of the literature on this topic with the following statement:

> The counselor is torn. He or she is formally told one thing about homosexuality from the profession (i.e., "homosexuality is okay"), and more informally, but no less persuasively, quite another from society-at-large ("homosexuality is not okay"). Support for this contention is provided by data indicating attitudes towards homosexuality in the adult population to be generally more consistently (albeit not exclusively) antigay in nature than is true of the attitudes of human service personnel (e.g., Gallup, 1977; National Opinion Research Center, 1985). Unlike human service professionals, those in the general population are not in the untenable position of having to serve two masters.

Counselors providing services to gay men often experience significant conflict around this issue. In the last decade the mental health profession has continued to engage the debate about the 1973 resolution. Conservative Christian groups have advocated for "conversion" or "reparative therapies" that promise to change orientation from gay to straight. However, the American Psychiatric Association, the American Psychological Association, the American Counseling Association, the National Association of Social

Workers, and other professional groups have condemned these approaches (Barret & Barzan, 1997). See Chapter Two for further discussion of this issue.

Unfortunately, few training programs even address the issue of providing mental health services to gay men and lesbians. As a mental health professional, you need to address the issues surrounding working with gay men as you would any other mental health issue; your first step in preparation is to assess your own attitudes. The beginning point in this task calls for you to examine your own feelings, thoughts, and fantasies related to same-sex eroticism. Given society's negative attitude toward homosexuality, the mere process of validating same-sex attraction may generate significant anxiety (McHenry & Johnson, 1993). If you are unable to get beyond your own fears surrounding homosexual thoughts and feelings, you should immediately refer the client to another clinician who is more gay-positive (Baron, 1996).

Typically the focus of counseling sessions with gay men and lesbians includes issues related to coming out, the client's own internalized homophobia, and developmental concerns resulting from insufficient socialization to homosexual subcultures. The client who is coming out will experience anxiety around feared rejection from family and friends as well as struggle with learning to prize his or her homosexuality. The successful integration of the homosexual aspects of personality with the client's broader life structure can become an arduous process that involves depression and anxiety as well as joy and relief.

Many homosexuals have been deprived of the socialization process that most adolescents experience during their high school years. Although Ellen Degeneres and Melissa Ethridge and their respective partners were positive role models for lesbian parenting and relationships, they stand in stark contrast to virtually no positive, public models of gay male relationships and parenting on which to build expectations. In addition, there are few gathering places for homosexual teenagers that provide a positive atmosphere for sexual development and intimacy. Many gay men deal with this deprivation by going through a delayed adolescence as part of their coming-out process. Their social lives have an atmosphere of intrigue and excitement one would normally associate with early adolescence. Falling in and out of love at the drop of a hat, they may worry excessively about the superficiality of their social network. Over time, these developmental issues will pass as the client undertakes a more complete integration of his or her sexuality into a unique pattern of living.

One barrier to the successful integration of homosexuality is the client's own internalized homophobia. His reporting anger and resentment toward friends and family members who do not readily accept his homosexuality may be a screen to avoid dealing with his acceptance of himself. Tom said,

> I would get so angry with my mother. She would write me these awful letters about how I was ruining her life and warning me not to bring my friends to see her. I tried so hard to explain what was happening. I just wanted her to understand. Finally one day my counselor said, "Maybe the real problem is your understanding, not hers." Until he said that I had not realized that I was afraid of myself and just projected all of my own fears onto my mother. How could she ever learn to accept me until I learned to do that for myself?

Another client, Henry, said, "I was so angry that my brothers and sisters did not want to know about my new life. When they came to visit me, I took them to a gay restaurant and bar. They made numerous negative jokes about men holding hands and dancing together and finally asked me to take them home. I decided I would never have anything to do with them again if they were going to be so critical of the way I live my life."

Eventually Henry learned that he was demanding that his family accept him but was himself unable to accept their somewhat normal discomfort in the homosexual world. Rather than rejoice over the gift they offered in going out with him, he blamed them for what was really his inability to maintain a positive gay identity when faced with negative comments. Such internalized homophobia is typical among gay men and lesbians as they come out.

There are no studies that report the experiences of gay fathers in therapy. But several investigations about the experiences of gay men and lesbians in the mental health system exist. Beane (1981) suggests that the task is to help the client develop a positive gay identity, a difficult undertaking in a society that is blatantly anti-gay. Helping the client reevaluate his personal values relative to homophobic introjection, gay male stereotypes, masculinity, and sexual activity and monogamy are central to the successful outcome of therapy. Some of your major tasks as a therapist include providing a safe place for the gay male who is coming out to have contact with himself, to rediscover his body and emotions, and to learn ways of supporting his often tentative positive gay identity. For many gay clients, the only place where they can discuss their sexuality without encountering society's fear and mistrust may be in your office. Helping the client find support in the community at large will be an important aspect of the treatment.

Decker (1984) identifies specific issues in counseling gay and lesbian couples. Many times you may be misled into thinking that the problems being presented are grounded in the couple's sexual orientation, when in fact the distress in these couple relationships can be traced to developmental issues and family dynamics that would cause similar difficulty in a heterosexual relationship. About the only thing unique about working with a gay or lesbian couple is the prevalence of boundary-related issues. For example, because our social systems often fail to validate the importance and permanence of the gay or lesbian relationship, the couple can become isolated and alienated from their families of origin and from aspects of the subculture. The tendency is for both members of the couple to expect a relationship that is perfect and satisfies every need. Naturally, integrating this relationship into the larger family of origin is a significant task and one that the couple may initiate.

If one or both members of the couple have come from an en-meshed family, there may be significant distress over intimacy is-sues. In short, the relationship may be troubled because of an insufficient amount of external support. The absence of shared chil-dren, legal sanction, and the prevailing single lifestyle focus within the gay subculture combine to present serious and often destructive obstacles for the gay and lesbian couple. Decker encourages coun-selors to spend significant time on family-of-origin issues, to care-fully look for unresolved coming-out issues, to be open to the way each couple constructs a unique model of a successful relationship, and to avoid imprinting the heterosexual marriage model on gay men and lesbians.

One gay father, Adam, said,

> When I was nineteen, I went to the most respected psychiatrist in my community and told him I thought I was gay. We talked a few times, and he told me, "Don't worry about it. This is just a phase. You are not sick like the queers you see on TV. You will grow out of it." I took his advice, and I started going out with women, got married, and found myself a father at age twenty-two. The attraction to men wouldn't go away, though, and after a few years I knew I had to be honest with myself. My wife left me when she found out, and I've not been allowed to even see my son since he was five years old. I know where he is now, and I suppose I could write to him. But I'm sure my ex-wife has poisoned him against me. I don't think there's any point in my messing up his life now. Maybe if he wants to find me, we will meet one day. I think about him a lot. That damn psychiatrist shares some of the blame for this. If he had just taken me seriously, I would never have married and had a son. I'll never trust a counselor again.

TIPS FOR PRACTITIONERS

Providing mental health services to gay fathers is a very complex task. The three major counseling issues gay fathers face are resolving the grief that accompanies any failed relationship, finding ways to acquire a new support system, and facing the potential rejection by children. Grieving the loss of heterosexuality and all the privileges attached to that life can be complicated and enduring. The prevalence and complexity of pain in each case can become overwhelming to both you and your client. It is not a task to be undertaken lightly.

Fortunately, there are some specific guidelines to assist you in your work with gay men and lesbians. Most clients will be quite patient and understanding with you if they realize you have not had experience with homosexual clients as long as you present yourself in a genuine manner and acknowledge your lack of intimate knowledge about the gay culture. If you behave in an empathic manner, offering clients a safe place to explore their feelings, they will be glad to teach you. We offer the following suggestions for the major issues you can anticipate.

Foster Self-Acceptance

When fathers are the primary clients, they often need positive support and encouragement as they begin to explore their sexual orientation. Usually this process involves turmoil and anxiety. The challenges involved in accepting self as gay can become so severe that the client may attempt suicide. You can assist the client in resolving this conflict by helping him accept himself for who he is and resolve the internalized negative stereotypes of homosexuality. Your clients will often achieve self-acceptance through disclosure and acceptance by loved ones. Of course, rejection is always a possibility for which gay fathers must prepare themselves.

Understand the Complexity of Adoption

Assisting gay couples who become fathers through adoption demands particular sensitivity. First, it is important to help the couple sort through a series of questions: How out are they willing to be as they interview agencies that handle adoptions? Who is going to be the legal father? Do they have a legal agreement about fathering rights and responsibilities and custody should the relationship fail? How will they inform and seek support from their extended families? In what ways might the adoption affect their relationship? Who will stay home when the child is sick or needs special care? Are they comfortable being out to health care workers and school personnel?

In some cases you will be the single professional who is equipped to assist with the couple's exploration of these unknowns. Your listening to them explain their plans and raising questions when appropriate will deepen their understanding about some of the issues ahead of them.

Deal with Ongoing Issues That Resurface

Coming out and developing a positive gay identity are lifelong tasks that may need periodic refinement. The gay and lesbian subculture is exceedingly rich and diverse, and it is probable that people will move through different aspects of it over time. A "phase of life" involved with bars and more superficial relationships can mature into a social life revolving around dinner gatherings, theater outings, and other activities that simply reflect the culture of the larger community.

Further, at significant family turning points it is not uncommon for gay fathers to re-experience grief over being gay. For instance, at family gatherings, such as marriages, family reunions, births, illnesses, or funerals, the client's homosexuality may become an issue that can trigger unresolved self-hatred and fear. Your client may report distress at revisiting these issues and can be helped by recalling that coming out is an ongoing process.

Although a gay man's coming out to his family does communicate the development of a positive gay identity, your expecting the client to disclose to his family before he is ready is inappropriate. Some gay men never come out to their families; their right to control who they tell may be the only thing that they feel they do control, and you must respect their choice.

Provide Network Opportunities

More specialized services are needed to meet the needs of gay men: some of them are still married or agonizing over divorce and custody issues, and others are still in the process of coming out and are struggling with identity concerns. Helping gay fathers establish social networks composed of both homosexuals and heterosexuals who accept both identities can help them resolve these conflicts. You can arrange group discussions, even if they involve only two gay fathers. Groups allow the men to share their pain, failures, joys, and successes and can be helpful, especially during the rough early days of coming out, resolving identity conflict, and separating from the children's mother. According to Mager (1975, p. 132), "Such meetings would break down the isolation, would bring the feeling of self-confidence, and would open up alternatives which a person might not think of."

This same process of integrative sanctioning—integrating positive feelings about being gay—(Bozett, 1981a, 1981b) is evident as the client begins to disclose his gay identity to heterosexuals and disclose his fathering role to other gay individuals. His worst fear may be that he does not belong in either world, creating an overwhelming sense of alienation. Supporting him as he identifies support within the larger community or in nearby communities can help ease this process. Gay father groups that meet in larger metropolitan areas offer a significant affirmation and a place to sort out some of the more pressing issues. Simply corresponding with one of these groups may ease some of the sense of isolation. Talking to other gay fathers and reading the scant literature on gay fathers also can be helpful. Finding gay neighborhoods, gay churches, and legal support organizations will be reassuring to the newly out gay father.

Thoughts of suicide sometimes accompany major life changes that involve loss and being out of control. Some gay fathers express their deep despair by talking about ending their lives. Although you

must take these threats seriously, your client's activating an extended support network will do much to lessen the feelings of alienation that often prompt such threats. For example, simply being able
to refer the client to other gay fathers in his community will provide testimony that will normalize the client's experience and foster his sense of inclusion and acceptance.

The Family Pride Coalition can serve as a source of social support for gay men and lesbians and their families. Contact with other
gay fathers through this organization can resolve feelings of isolation and alienation and help in conflict resolution. This organization
provides an opportunity for gay fathers to unite, despite their varied experiences, to help each other integrate the two aspects of their
lives. The coalition's overriding belief is that gay men and lesbians
can love and nourish children and provide a safe environment in
which their kids can mature into loving and productive men and
women. The organization was originally formed to help gay men
grow and develop and draw on the rich experience of both aspects
of their lives. They achieve this through mutually supportive groups
for building a positive self-image and for creative problem solving.
The coalition locates other gay men who are fathers, are contem-
plating fatherhood, or may be struggling alone. It also educates professionals and the general public about the special concerns related
to being a gay parent.

Refrain from Premature Labeling

The father who has been deeply closeted may prematurely rush to
label himself as gay, when in fact he may actually have more of a bisexual orientation. Such premature labeling and disclosure can create major difficulties. Some clients may see identifying as gay as a
way to relieve their anxiety about who they are. Labeling self as gay
or bisexual may be appropriate only after the man's life has settled
into a more familiar pattern. In cautioning your client against premature self-labeling, you must create a gay-positive atmosphere; it

is essential that the client perceive this "warning" as an expression of concern for his well-being rather than as simply one more homophobic response.

You will find helping gay fathers work through these issues rewarding. As time passes and the family recovers from its initial loss, all family members can experience significant growth. Of course, not all families will completely incorporate their loved one's sexual orientation, but many come to realize that being gay is just one aspect of the person they love, and they find that they have a new relationship based on a stronger sense of integrity and respect.

2

Gay Fathers
Myths and Realities

Robin left his wife just over a year after their daughter, Tyler, was born. Faced with a demanding job and the task of building a new life, his major focus was on his daughter.

I remember sitting in church with my eighteen-month-old daughter asleep in my arms and a guy I had begun to date sitting to my left when my estranged wife's lawyer came and sat down in the pew to my right. At that point my wife did not know why I had asked for a separation. I wasn't prepared for her to find out this way. Nor did I think I was ready for the agony that I was sure lay ahead of me. Over the past two years I had been faced with so many of my lifelong fears. My greatest one was that my wife, her lawyer, our families, and God would work together to take my child from me. I went home from church that day and rocked my child in my arms as if it would be the last time, and tears fell from my eyes.

You see, my story is not unlike many gay fathers. For years I had spent my life struggling to live within the given social norms, or what I have come to call a white-picket-fence life. I was the model son, a devoted brother, a committed church member, a loving husband, and, I hoped, a good father. It was as if in filling these roles I could give myself some sort of reprieve or redemption from what I hid underneath. I just knew that these people would not love me if they knew I was gay.

Becoming a father was a turning point for me. The life I had so carefully crafted began to unravel. There were feelings and yearnings or whatever you want to call them that just would not leave me alone. I have always tried to live an honorable life. I have always tried to be honest with myself and with those around me. I didn't know what to do with these new and misunderstood feelings. Being gay and acting on those feelings just was not on my list and threatened to destroy the picture I had painted of my future. Regardless of the efforts of those around me, I began to slip away. I became emotionally uninvolved in the daily activities that took place around me. I slipped into a depression that would often leave me incapable of getting off the couch. I felt more alone than ever before in my life, and the future became very dark.

No one could convince me that I needed help. I had to reach that decision on my own. Finally I made an appointment with a psychologist, and, for the first time, told someone else that I am a homosexual. I fully expected him to ridicule me for being gay and especially for being married, and most decidedly for fathering a child. I had convinced myself that I was the absolute worst person in the world, and I was not going to be easily convinced otherwise. But slowly I began to realize that my homosexuality was not a choice, and that blaming and shaming myself for being gay was like blaming a leopard for its spots. Being gay is not right or wrong; it just is who I am. I also came to realize that being gay did not reduce me to a one-dimensional creature with no more complexity than my sexual orientation.

We celebrated Tyler's fifth birthday last week. My mother and two sisters were there, as well as my niece and nephew. Michael, the guy who was in church with me, has grown from the "someone I was beginning to date" into my life partner. His mother, father, sister, and two nieces came to the party too. Bob, another gay father, came with his son. Two straight couples in our neighborhood were there with their children. Michael, Tyler, and I spent a week at the beach with one of these families last summer and have plans to go back again this summer. Each of these people is integrated into Michael's and my life with Tyler. My daughter is exposed to a variety of people with a variety of life experiences to offer her.

If you had told me three-and-a-half years ago, when I sat in that church desperately trying not to run away and never stop, that my life would be where it is today, I would not have believed you. There have been a lot of milestones along the way. The first time I saw my ex-wife's family was when I picked up Tyler from their house one Christmas Eve. I was sure my reception would be far colder than the weather outside. My ex-mother-in-law answered the door, gave me a big hug, and whispered in my ear that it was going to be OK. Believe me, hearing that OK was the greatest Christmas present I could have received. Tyler saw me and yelled, "Look everybody, Daddy's here!" My ex-wife's family was extremely gracious then and continues to be now.

Tyler's mother still considers homosexuality to be wrong and sinful. Fortunately, she believes that our daughter needs her father. Michael and I have Tyler with us every other weekend. Typically, since Michael works in the same general area as where my ex-wife lives, he will pick Tyler up to bring her to our home. She isn't quite sure how Michael fits into the family. Once she asked me if he was my friend, and I thought, "Oh, brother, here it comes." Somehow she knows that "friend" doesn't exactly explain my relationship with him. Since her mother remarried last year, I told her that just as her step-dad is important to her mother, so Michael is important to me. She looked away for a moment as if to filter that thought through her four-year-old world of experience and then said, "OK." She turned back to her dress-up clothes and became the Princess-of-the-World. At this point in her life, she may not fully understand, but she treats Michael as a member of the family. For someone who never wanted kids, he has taken to parenting amazingly well. It is apparent that he loves her and that she returns his affection. I still get nervous thinking about what I will tell her when she gets older. I know I will have to talk with her mother before discussing it in depth with Tyler.

When we have Tyler over on weekends, we try to spend that time as a family. We have gotten baby-sitters occasionally, but I don't really like leaving Tyler. Michael and I have dinner with her at least once during the week, and she is old enough now so we can visit on the phone. Michael and I have gone as a couple to the Christmas program at her school. He has taken her to school and picked her up as well. I have volunteered in her classroom and attend PTA meetings. We are treated like any other couple who loves their child. We look, act, and feel like a family. We are fortunate to have met other gay men and lesbians who have children. It has been extremely helpful to talk with others who have or are presently going through the same life experiences as we are. The children who are Tyler's age come over to play. I think that as she grows, it will be important for her to have friends who have gay and lesbian parents too.

We have faced very little adversity in our journey. The things that have happened have been hurtful, though. Michael's sister asked that we not sleep in the same bed when her children spend the night. That came as a shock. Until that point our families had been so supportive and had treated us no differently than when we were living with our wives. Michael's parents treat Tyler as another grandchild. Michael tried to explain to his sister that what she was asking of us would communicate to Tyler that something was wrong with our family. We would not send that message to her. Finally, we decided that her children would not spend the night in our home. Tyler loves to play with them, and I dread the time when she asks if they can spend the night.

One thing I keep trying to work out is our spiritual life. When my ex-wife and I were married, we were active in our church. We taught Sunday school and were officers of the congregation. I want to play a part in Tyler's religious education but so far have not been able to find the church that feels right for us. The MCC [gay church] is not a place I would join even if I were not a father. We've gone to the uptown

Episcopal and Methodist churches and know they would welcome us along with all others. We even went to a small inner-city Presbyterian church made up of people of many races, sexual orientations, and family configurations. None of these have offered what I hope to find. Lately we have been attending a liberal Baptist church and are leaning toward joining. They have a strong children's program, and the church leadership has encouraged us to join as the church's first gay family. It may be a little too cutting-edge for me, though, since it is a congregation that has not fully decided that gay men and lesbians are welcome equally.

There are plenty of unknowns ahead for us. I used to think that I could prepare for any eventuality. Now I don't worry about the unknowns as much. I don't have to have all the answers. Someone once told me that not all decisions are right or wrong ones. Some decisions are simply the best decision we make at the time with what we know to be honest and true. I have spent quite a lot of energy over my lifetime trying to make the right decisions. Now I am trying to concentrate on making the best decision I can with what I know to be true and honest. I oftentimes wish that I had the proverbial crystal ball so that I could see Tyler grown up. I know that having a gay father will add complexity to her life. I also know that the best way to prepare her for her journey is to surround her with as much love as possible today. Love that is true and honest. I wrote her a letter trying to explain what had led me to live the life I now lead. Two sentences from that letter best describe what I wish for her: "I want you to see your father as a whole man who is happy with who he is. Most of all, I want you to see a father who truly loves his child." Our family may not be traditional, but we are a family.

Robin
Charlotte, North Carolina

MYTHS AND RESEARCH

Throughout this book, we document scientific findings, our own as well as others, with anecdotal material that we have collected from gay fathers over the years. In our studies we discovered numerous myths that are generally held about these men. Noted anthropologist Ashley Montagu (1978, p. 91) believes such myths derive from stereotypes and misinformation: "Homosexuality is not a problem that homosexuals create."

The definitive understanding of the origins of homosexuality continues to elude us. Studies on etiology examine family background, twins, early gender-discordant behavior, and genetics (Marmor, 1998). LeVay (1991) compared the brains of gay men who had died from HIV disease with samples of brain tissue from deceased men who identified as heterosexual, and found that a region in the anterior hypothalamus was smaller in the tissues obtained from the gay men, suggesting a possible biological basis to sexual orientation. As yet he has not been successful in obtaining samples from gay men who died of other causes, so there is no conclusive evidence that homosexuality can be seen in the structure of the brain. More and more researchers, however, are beginning to attribute sexual orientation to genetics or to the result of a genetic predisposition that is enhanced by unknown environmental factors (LeVay & Hamer, 1994). The important point is that the jury is still out about why some men and women become homosexuals. But few serious professionals believe it is a choice. Let's take a look at some of the myths about homosexuality and see how they create challenges for gay fathers.

- Disturbed parental relationships myth: Homosexuals, including gay fathers, have disturbed parental relationships (for example, cold, rejecting fathers and emotionally smothering mothers) that cause them to become attracted to same-sex partners.
- Macho myth: Gay fathers capable of having sex with a female are more masculine than gay men in general.
- Germ myth: Interactions between gay fathers and their children will lead to transmission of homosexuality to the offspring. Children of homosexual fathers will turn out to be homosexual themselves.

- Harassment exposure myth: Gay fathers expose their children to harassment and embarrassment because of societal disapproval.
- Molestation myth: There is a high incidence of sexual abuse among children of gay fathers. Gay men in general and gay fathers in particular sexually exploit unsuspecting children.
- Sex-fiend myth: The main goal in life for gay fathers is primarily that of sexual gratification.
- Smoke screen myth: Gay men become fathers as a cover to hide their homosexuality so they can function more easily in society.
- Compensation myth: Gay men enter into heterosexual relationships and have children to compensate for and deny their homosexual feelings.
- Identification myth: Homosexual men marry and become fathers in order to identify with the feelings and the feminine roles of their wives.
- Sick myth: Gay fathers are psychologically sick and need therapy to help them change their sexual orientation so that it is more compatible with their fathering role.

Many of these myths emerged because there have been so few scientific studies conducted on gay fathers and because, until recently, the invisibility of gay men allowed the myths to flourish unchallenged. From 1974 to the present, as researchers began to realize the important roles fathers play in their children's development, and with the advent of changing sex roles and a greater acceptance of homosexuality among professional organizations, "the age of gay parenthood" has emerged from the closet and conversations about the "gayby boom" are becoming more common. Men like Robin strongly refute the image most people hold about gay fathers. The information unearthed from research studies debunks each of the aforementioned myths about gay fathers and helps us gain a better understanding of their plight than professionals have held in the past.

Our main theme throughout our research on homosexuality and the family has been the nature of the relationships between gay fathers and their families and friends. Our interest in this subject began with a national study on gay men's and women's perceptions of their early family lives and how they saw their relationships with parents. Those positive findings refuted the stereotype of a sick family history as a necessary condition for homosexuality to occur. This caused us to question many of the other myths that surround homosexuality and to examine the gay father's role more closely.

A National Study

One of the first national studies of gay men and lesbian women was conducted in 1982 (Robinson, Skeen, Flake-Hobson, & Herrman, 1982). The authors were interested in knowing about the early family lives of gay men and their relationships with their parents. The questionnaire consisted of three sections. The first section included demographic information. The second section assessed current relationship status and asked respondents to answer yes or no to such questions as, "Are you currently living with someone? Yes (roommate), yes (lover, opposite sex), yes (lover, same sex), or no." Other questions concerned whether respondents had previously lived with someone, their current marital status, and whether they had any children. The third and main section of the questionnaire contained thirteen items. Five of them measured respondents' perceptions of their mothers' acceptance (Mother Acceptance Scale) and five measured perceptions of their fathers' acceptance (Father Acceptance Scale). Items included acceptance of the child's being homosexual, description of the relationship with parent, whether the respondent felt loved by his or her parent, the respondent's ability to live up to parent's expectations, and how the parent would rate the respondent's worthiness as a child. Respondents were asked to react to such questions as, "How would you describe your relationship with your mother?" with Likert-scale responses (on a scale from one to five, extremely unsatisfactory to extremely satisfactory). Three additional items dealt with family atmosphere during childhood. On a five-point scale, respondents rated degree of marital discord during their upbringing and degree of pleasantness of their childhood until and during adolescence. They were asked if both parents were present in the house during their upbringing, and if not, which parent was absent.

In order to locate as diverse a sample as possible, the researchers surveyed five regions of the country: 25 percent from the Northeast; 15 percent from the Midwest, 33 percent from the South, 18 percent from the Southwest; and 9 percent from the West. They contacted all seventy-two chapters of Dignity, an organization composed of gay men and lesbian women from all denominations and religious preferences. Dignity's purpose is to work for the support and acceptance of gay men and women and to elicit responsive approaches from society as a whole. They mailed questionnaires to all Dignity chapters across the United States that had previously expressed a willingness to participate. Each group leader, who had been given instructions for completing the forms during a regular meeting, distributed questionnaires. The total number of returned forms was 332 (285 men and 47 women), a return rate of 62 percent.

Findings revealed that two-thirds of the sample perceived their relationships with their fathers as extremely satisfactory or satisfactory. Over three-fourths perceived their relationships with their mothers as extremely satisfactory or satisfactory. The majority perceived that both their fathers and mothers would accept their homosexuality. Although relationships with mothers were perceived to be slightly better than relationships with fathers, both maternal and paternal parent-child relationships were described more as adequate and positive than as inadequate or negative.

Disturbed Parental Relationships Myth

The authors of the study were particularly interested in understanding the disturbed parental relationship myth surrounding gay fathers and their early parental interactions. The intriguing findings from the national homosexual population compelled them to go a step further and analyze a subsample of responses from gay fathers in the study (Skeen & Robinson, 1984). This turned out to be thirty men, or approximately 10 percent of the sample, who had fathered one or more children. Children of gay fathers ranged in age from one to thirty-four years. The fathers represented five regions of the country: from the Northeast, 13 percent; Midwest, 23 percent; South, 23 percent; Southwest, 27 percent; and West, 13 percent. All but one father had at one time been involved in a heterosexual marriage. The profile of early family backgrounds of gay fathers emerging from the data was generally positive. It was not possible to determine from this study what effect (if any) the positive early family experiences had on gay fathers' decisions to become involved in heterosexual marriage and to father children, as no questions dealt with this issue. But most gay fathers grew up in intact homes where heterosexual relationships were modeled for them and marital discord was uncommon, and about which the men hold pleasant memories. Although respondents perceived their relationship with their mother to be slightly better than that with father, they described both maternal and paternal parent-child relationships more as adequate and positive than as inadequate and negative.

Most gay fathers also believed that both their mothers and fathers viewed them as worthy individuals, although mothers did so slightly more than fathers. Overall, the findings refuted the old psychoanalytic myth that disturbed parental relationships are necessary and sufficient conditions for gay fathers. In fact, gay fathers seemed to value stability of family relationships from childhood into their adult lives. Asked, "What important things do you want to accomplish in your lifetime?" responses dealt with stabilizing family relationships (50 percent), having a successful career (33 percent), and improving the lot of homosexuals in general (17 percent). One father responded: "Wisdom to tell my children (at the right age) what loving another man means to me—emotionally, mentally, spiritually, but not necessarily physically." Asked, "What thing or things are most important to you in your life right now?" recurrent themes were children, partners, careers, religion, peace of mind, and health. Practically all fathers had dissolved their heterosexual marriages in favor of homosexual relationships, and many fathers listed both their children and partners as important in their lives. Typical responses were these: "my two children, a new male friend"; "son, job, relationship"; "building my relationship with my daughter, parents, and lover"; "my children, parents, and church"; "being more accepted by my children."

To carry the data analysis a step further, a matched sample of gay nonfathers was compared with the group of gay fathers, with particular emphasis on parent-son relationships (Skeen & Robinson, 1985). The findings were similar to those discussed earlier involving the entire sample. No difference was found between gay fathers' and gay nonfathers' perceptions of their parents' acceptance of them. Both groups perceived their mothers to be more accepting than their fathers. The majority of gay fathers (24 of 30) and nonfathers (23 of 30) had grown up in intact families with both mother and father present. Contrary to long-held psychoanalytic beliefs that homosexuals' families are characterized by negative relationships and abnormality, the majority of both gay fathers and nonfathers viewed their families as primarily pleasant and without much discord.

The finding that gay fathers and nonfathers both view their mothers as more accepting than their fathers is interesting. It could be construed to support the Freudian idea that homosexuals' relationships with their fathers are unsatisfactory, characterized by coldness, rejection, and absences, whereas homosexuals are overly close to their mothers. However, because most of the sample viewed their relationship with their fathers as primarily positive, this explanation seems implausible. A more reasonable explanation may be related to child-rearing practices in general. The men in this sample were likely to have experienced a traditional upbringing, growing up in families in which mothers were the primary caretakers and fathers the economic providers. As a result of this parenting pattern, heterosexual as well as homosexual children are more likely to feel closer to (that is, more loved, accepted, and valued by) their mothers than their fathers. Taken together, these findings refute the Freudian-based concept of a causal relationship between early family relationship patterns and sexual orientation.

Macho Myth

Traditionally, our society has perpetuated the stereotype that homosexual men are more feminine than heterosexual men and that lesbian women are more masculine than heterosexual women. This stereotype has been refuted by numerous studies that show masculinity and femininity among homosexuals to be unrelated to their sexual lifestyles and that the stereotype of cross-gender endorsement is unfounded (Storms, 1980). Just as femininity and male homosexuality have been connected, there has also been a tendency to link two other unrelated phenomena: masculinity and fatherhood. Here is how a gay father expressed his perception of this myth: "Being a father and a gay man are incompatible. Here I suddenly am as a father and that automatically meant I must not be gay. There was a piece of that when I got married; I thought that somehow if I were married I would not be gay. It was sort of like when my wife got pregnant the first time, I thought, 'Well, I am a man, and I'm not gay.' If you can propagate, you're masculine. You're not 'weird' or gay."

The macho myth implies that gay fathers, because they may have been married, have had sexual intercourse with the opposite sex, and have fathered children, are more masculine than gay men who do not enter into these relationships. This myth was put to the test by comparing two groups, one of gay fathers and the other of gay nonfathers, on sex-role orientation (Robinson & Skeen, 1982). The Bem Sex Role Inventory (Bem, 1974) was administered to all participants in the national study (as described earlier), along with

Table 2.1. Frequencies of Gay Men Who Scored Androgynous, Masculine, Feminine, or Undifferentiated

	Androgynous	Masculine	Feminine	Undifferentiated	Total
Fathers	9	5	8	8	30
Nonfathers	7	8	6	9	30
Totals	16	13	14	17	60

the questionnaire. Findings did not support the myth that gay fathers are any more masculine than gay men who do not father children. As Table 2.1 shows, a pattern of diverse sex-role orientation was found in which gay men scored equally often masculine, feminine, androgynous (blending both masculine and feminine traits), and undifferentiated, regardless of whether or not they had fathered children. The results indicated that gay fathers and gay nonfathers as a group can be described as more nonandrogynous (that is, either masculine, feminine, or undifferentiated) than androgynous, although fewer fathers scored masculine than in any other category. This finding debunks the myth that masculinity is a prerequisite for fatherhood among gay men and suggests that sexual behavior and sex-role orientation are unrelated phenomena that develop out of separate experiences.

Germ Myth

Perhaps the biggest misunderstanding about gay fathers is that they will transmit their homosexuality, deliberately or inadvertently, to their children. The germ myth is related to homophobia—an emotional reaction of deep-seated revulsion and fear toward homosexuals and their lifestyles (Weinberg, 1972). The stereotype that exposure to a gay person will cause one to become homosexual has been generalized from the homosexual population at large to gay fathers and their offspring. A social worker who is employed in specialized care for behaviorally and emotionally disabled children reported common homophobic reactions from the staff:

A lot of helping professionals, especially men, are afraid that a gay father will seduce them, recruit them, or make some pass at them. They're afraid they're going to catch homosexuality. They don't understand it and think that contact with a gay man will dirty or soil them in some way. Even before the AIDS epidemic, I observed the staff's fear of being contaminated by homosexuals. One staff member said of a gay father in a psychiatric hospital where I worked, "The dad is coming to visit this weekend. I'm glad you're working this weekend and not me." It was like a hot potato that nobody wanted to handle. Recently, after an AIDS seminar at our facility the secretary came in and cleaned her office with Clorox. Although nobody with AIDS had been there, the topic so scared her as a result of the seminar that she was not going to take any chances.

The truth is that most children of homosexual men and women turn out to be heterosexual (Cramer, 1986). Only about 10 percent of the offspring develop homosexual identities (Bailey, Bobrow, Wolfe, & Mikach, 1995). Our own research with 702 parents of homosexual men and women indicates that 90 percent of the parents are heterosexual, 4 percent bisexual, and only 6 percent completely homosexual (Robinson, Walters, & Skeen, 1989). One father we spoke with said, "My parents are heterosexual, but I turned out to be gay. So why would anyone believe my homosexuality would rub off on my son?" Another father told us, "I don't believe that if I have questions about myself that my son or daughter will have questions about themselves. I certainly didn't question my sexuality because my father or brothers questioned theirs. If they did, I never knew it. I can't see anywhere in my family where anyone else is gay. Nobody has ever approached me sexually or molested me. Never, ever, has anything like that happened to me, and yet I have these feelings. So I don't believe there's any contamination going on. I am whatever I am for whatever reasons I will never know."

Brian Miller (1979a) assessed the sexual orientation of the twenty-seven daughters and twenty-one sons of forty gay fathers from cities across the United States and Canada. All the fathers were white, mostly middle class and college educated, and they ranged in age from twenty-four to sixty-four. According to the fathers' report, only 8 percent of the children were gay (one of the sons and three of the daughters). Although Miller's study was not randomized, second-generation homosexuals were rare in this sample. Psychiatrist Richard Green (1978) studied thirty-seven children, ranging in age from three to twenty, who were being raised by female homosexuals or by male and female parents who had sex-change surgery. After two years of study, thirty-six out of the thirty-seven children showed clear heterosexual preferences or were developing them. Thirteen adolescent children were attracted to the opposite sex. Green concluded, "The children I interviewed were able to comprehend and verbalize the atypical nature of their parent's lifestyles and to view their atypicality in the broader perspective of the cultural norm" (p. 696). Thus, the homophobic myth that children will be contaminated by their gay fathers is unfounded. A study by the Kinsey Institute of Sex Research concluded from a sample of one thousand homosexuals and five hundred heterosexuals that sexual preference results from many factors but begins with an early, probably biological, tendency toward homosexuality or heterosexuality (Bell, Weinberg, & Hammersmith, 1981).

Harassment Exposure Myth

The harassment myth holds that gay fathers expose their children to ridicule and embarrassment because they place their sexual desires above the welfare of their kids. There is an element of truth to this myth. When gay fathers are open about their sexuality, their children sometimes face harassment from peers and other adults. Research shows, however, that gay fathers are sensitive to the accompanying problems of being the child of a gay parent. In cases where fathers openly identify as gay, they ordinarily prepare their children early to deal with ridicule, or they take extra precautions to protect their kids from harassment (Bozett, 1980). Other gay fathers help their children deal with harassment by teaching them about tolerance of others. There is a tendency for gay fathers to instill accepting and nonjudgmental attitudes toward all human beings, regardless of race, religious beliefs, or sexual orientation. "If Eryn is gay, he should, unlike his father, have healthy gay role models to preserve him from self-hatred and isolation," says one gay father about his son. "If he is straight, he should have learned tolerance of sexual variation" (quoted in Fadiman, 1983, p. 80).

Molestation Myth

The molestation myth suggests that gay fathers, because of their same-sex attraction, will molest their sons or other children. It further implies that their same-sex attraction is the primary motivating factor in their lives. A social worker told us that there happened to be a sex offender on the unit of a psychiatric hospital where he worked. At the same time, a child had been admitted for chemical dependency. The child's father was gay, and the staff equated the gay father with the sex offender who had molested a child. Although this is a common association, the research and statistical data strongly show that this belief is wrong. According to national police statistics, sexual abuse of children is a heterosexual crime in 90 percent of the cases (Voeller & Walters, 1978). Social science research also indicates that sexual exploitation of children by their homosexual parents is virtually nonexistent (Miller, 1979a). One study concludes that "the adult heterosexual male constitutes a greater sexual risk to underage children than does the adult homosexual male" (Groth & Birnbaum, 1978, p. 181).

Sex-Fiend Myth

A pervasive myth about gay fathers and homosexuals in general is that sex is all they think about and do. Sexual energy governs their lives, and they are slaves to their uncontrollable sexual urges. What is not understood is that gay men engage in sexual activity equally as often as their heterosexual counterparts. Being gay refers to a whole approach to life, of which being sexually intimate is but one small part. Gay men are viewed suspiciously around children, but especially around boys. Gay men are perceived as having fleeting and superficial relationships and being incapable of committed relationships. Generalized to gay fathers, the sex-fiend myth was described by a father struggling with his own sexual identity:

There is this widespread notion that gay men cannot sustain relationships and tend to be very self-centered. Most of their relationships are fleeting and troubled. The ability to have a positive relationship as a parent would seem to contradict that myth. The notion of a gay man sacrificing his own immediate pleasure for his children sounds contradictory because sexuality is viewed as the prime motivator for gay men. Part of it too is a general belief that gay men would expose their kids to a lot of open sex and are sexually promiscuous and not concerned about how their children view that. If one accepted that myth, then the notion of being committed as a father and being willing to sacrifice as a father would seem unusual.

Smoke Screen Myth

The moving case of Robin in itself is convincing evidence that the incompatibility of being both father and homosexual is not a conscious, deceitful act. Still, this popular belief haunts him: "I worry that when I tell my old friends that I'm gay they'll respect me less and say, 'Well, you're a person who has lived a lie all these years. How dare you come to me for support when all these years you've been hiding?' That hasn't happened yet. The people I've talked to have been very accepting and willing to let me just be where I am."

The smoke screen myth holds that gay men use their marriages and children to conceal their true sexual orientation and to gain society's acceptance. A newspaper article by Beth Krier (1988) titled "America's Becoming Single-Minded" perpetuated the smoke screen myth as a common phenomenon—so common that the growing number of openly gay men was offered as one reason for the rise in single adults: "Some experts suspect that, as society becomes more accepting of alternative lifestyles, fewer homosexuals feel the need to marry to hide their sexual orientation" (p. 6D).

In contrast to this myth, both our clinical experience and the emerging research indicate that most gay men enter into hetero-sexual relationships and fatherhood with an honest and authentic desire for successful family relationships and not out of a desire to mask their homosexuality. Recent data comparing gay and straight fathers' attitudes and motivations for fatherhood reveal that in both groups, marriages and family orientations reflect a traditional atti-tude toward family life (Bigner & Jacobsen, 1989b). Another study of thirty-two gay fathers found three major reasons why these men married. In descending order the reasons were (1) love of the pro-spective spouse, (2) personal and social expectations, and (3) hope that marriage would rid them of their homosexuality (Wyers, 1987). Although the majority of gay fathers (68.6 percent) in that study knew or suspected they were homosexual at or before the time of marriage, many men do not fully discover their homosexuality until after they marry.

Other research shows that at the time of marriage many fathers do not think of themselves as homosexual (Miller, 1979a). Even those fathers who had already had sex with other men before mar-riage considered themselves as heterosexual or bisexual. They en-tered marriage with a genuine love for their wives and a desire to have children. During the course of their marriages, they reported a conflict between the duality of fatherhood and homosexual awak-enings that eventually led to an exclusively homosexual orientation (Dank, 1972; Miller, 1978).

Compensation Myth

This is another misconception widely held by people in general. A common prescription for the "ills of homosexuality" is "a good lay" with a woman. Heterosexual sex and having kids, so it is widely be-lieved, will compensate for the homosexual feelings and thus "cure" gay men. A gay father of two children debunked that myth: "I had some of the greatest sex you can have with a woman. I was twenty-one dating a woman who was thirty-one. We'd go to bed on Friday and not get up until Sunday afternoon. As far as sex goes, it was great! But as far as my emotional needs and feelings—that 'something' you can only get from another man if you're gay—wasn't there. But coming from a heterosexual background, I thought, 'Well I guess this is what sex with women is all about. This is the way it's supposed to be.'"

Identification Myth

Another myth that stems from the psychoanalytic tradition posits unconscious motives for explaining why a homosexual man marries and has children is his burning desire to identify with his wife's feminine role. The following passage was presented in a psychiatric journal on a discussion of unmarried fathers:

> After convincing the woman she should marry him, the man turned against her and treated her and the child very sadistically. In all such cases there is some evidence that strong latent homosexual feelings exist in which the good relationship depends upon how much participation the man is permitted in the feelings of the woman. If these are such that he desires vicarious homosexual satisfaction in fantasies, by participating with her in her past life, the situation may be very tolerable. If this does not work out because of too much excitement, the man ends up leaving the woman or treating her miserably [Reider, 1948, p. 234].

Sick Myth

There is still a pervasive attitude in today's society that views homosexuals and gay fathers as sick and in need of treatment. Pioneer psychoanalytic studies of the 1960s characterized homosexuals, particularly married gay men, as pathological (for example, Bieber, 1962). These early studies, riddled with methodological problems and investigator bias, have been severely criticized (Hooker, 1969). Bieber (1962), for example, studied male adult homosexuals and heterosexuals under psychiatric examination for various problems. Considering that these clients were already under treatment, it is not surprising that Bieber found pathological themes in his subjects. Bieber's study was further questioned because the analysts who were called on to furnish information regarding the data knew in which category the patient fell (that is, either homosexual or heterosexual), thus biasing the observers' opinions and contaminating research results.

These early studies that judged homosexuals to be sick prescribed a changed sexual orientation as a "cure." Today the medical, political, familial, and legal views are more tolerant of gay rights and lifestyles. More research and increased gay political clout have contributed to a better understanding of homosexuality and to changes in the attitudes of political groups as well as professional mental health organizations.

HOMOSEXUALITY AND REPARATIVE THERAPY

The origins of homosexuality continue to be obscure. Ever since the APA depathologized homosexuality and eliminated it from the *DS III*, there has been a steady stream of official positions taken by the leading mental health organizations affirming that being gay or lesbian does not equal being "sick." The APA, the National Association for Social Workers, the American Counseling Association, and others have taken official positions stating that any form of discrimination against gay men and lesbians is inappropriate and unprofessional. Accordingly, most psychologists, social workers, and counselors know that the standard of care in the treatment of gay clients involves taking a positive or at least neutral position toward clients' sexual orientation. Still, prejudicial practice is not unusual. In spite of the many articles (Fassinger, 1991; McHenry & Johnson, 1993) that review the negative impact of such counseling, Garnets, Hancock, Cochran, Goodchilds, and Peplau (1991) reported that negative attitudes persist among the 99 percent of mental health practitioners who provide services to gay men or lesbians. Thus, improving counseling services to sexual minorities continues to be a goal of professional groups.

In summer 1998, several conservative Christian groups took out full-page ads in the *New York Times, USA Today*, and other newspapers, proclaiming that homosexuality could be "cured." These ads featured men and women who described themselves as "ex-gays" who were now happily married. They heralded the success of both conversion therapy, a Christian-oriented approach, and reparative therapy, as championed by the National Association for Reparative Therapy for Homosexuals (NARTH). NARTH's founder, Joseph Nicolosi (1991), believes that men become gay because of an unsuccessful identification with their fathers. According to his theory, gay men seek out other men for sex as a reenactment of their frustrated desire for intimacy with their fathers. Although condemned by the major mental health associations, Nicolosi's work continues to receive attention.

Despite the persistence of groups such as NARTH and the condemnation of gay men and lesbians by conservative Christian leaders such as Jerry Falwell and Pat Robertson, the APA (1997) passed resolutions that emphasize the tenets of informed consent, especially in regard to the treatment of sexual orientation. These resolutions, which were devised in response to the lack of scientific evidence indicating that reparative or conversion therapy is effective, state that for practitioners to be seen as exercising the most ethical and professional care, they must inform prospective clients that there is no empirical research indicating that attempts to change sexual orientation can be successful. In December 1998, the APA went even further and declared that there are significant negative risks involved in attempts to change sexual orientation. In spring 1999, the American Counseling Association passed a similar resolution. Consumers of these treatments report that they were not told the truth about this approach and that they were assailed with statements that characterized homosexuals as lonely, unhappy, and unsuccessful. The bottom line is that conversion and reparative therapies emphasize a moral or value position that is not supported by scientific research (Markowitz, 1999). In short, homosexuality is not something that needs to be "fixed."

TIPS FOR PRACTITIONERS

The literature suggests that practitioners have paid little attention to the needs of homosexuals in general and to gay parents in particular. Homophobia pervades the very professions that are committed to helping fellow human beings. Homophobic attitudes and lack of awareness are obstacles to treatment and frequently circumvent gay father families from seeking treatment altogether. The legal system as well as social service agencies continue to operate and deliver services based on myths and stereotypes. For these reasons it is especially important that practitioners be aware of practicing without these harmful mind-sets.

Examine Your Prejudices

As we discussed in Chapter One, in order to work with gay fathers effectively, you must examine your own homophobic prejudices toward homosexuality and gay fathering. Where such biases exist, you can acknowledge and confront them. Recognizing uncomfortable feelings can be a valuable lesson, and you can deal with such feelings by gaining more information about gay marriages and lifestyles, thus erasing your prejudices. A practitioner told us, "Professionals need more training to better understand what the gay lifestyle is all about. They cling to a lot of myths—like the child molester myth or 'a good lay will solve your problems'—that get in the way of the real problems and do more harm than good." It is important for you to familiarize yourself with such issues as coming out, divorce, parenting problems, discrimination, and child custody. You can do this in individual counseling or through participation in psychoeducational groups. Learning to identify ways sexual attraction will influence the counseling relationship, developing a sensitivity to the often subtle discriminations that are communicated through language, and acquiring information about the subculture will enable you to get started much more confidently. It is not sufficient to know a few gay men and lesbians; you will need to take a more systematic approach to raising your awareness.

Talks with married gay men with whom you can make contact or discussions with colleagues who have had experiences working with homosexual couples or married gay men can help. Visits to gay bars, churches, or gay support organizations can be especially valuable. Many organizations also provide speakers for classrooms, churches, or professional organizations. You can draw on the resources in the Appendix. Listed are professional organizations established to prohibit discrimination toward clients on the basis of sexual orientation. You can use the Appendix as a resource bank for gay clients who have accepted their sexuality and wish to meet others to share their interests and concerns. Your enlightened response would be of great value to gay fathers as they attempt to resolve the pain and emotional upheaval in their marriages (Wyers, 1987). More enlightened responses are also needed from organizations offering specialized gay and lesbian services; some of these organizations still do not understand or address the unique needs of gay father families. In situations where helping practitioners (whether gay or straight) cannot resolve their prejudices, they should withdraw from the helping role when gay-father clients and their families are involved.

Use Appropriate Terminology

The parents of a gay son were horrified when their counselor referred to their son's homosexuality as "being that way" and for two sessions not once used the terms *gay* or *homosexual*. It turned out that the counselor was afraid the parents were not familiar with the term *gay child* and avoided it for fear of offending them; ironically, she ended up offending them anyway for not using proper words. Learning to use appropriate language is just one step in creating a successful therapeutic environment. Make sure you know and use contemporary terms when working with gay parents. The term *gay* is generally preferred to that of *homosexual*. Whereas the term *gay* often communicates an attitude of positive self-acceptance, referring to "gays" as a group is generally viewed negatively. Homosexual women often prefer to be referred to as *lesbian*.

Clarify and Validate the Client's Reality

It is critical that you help fathers clarify and validate their realities when they confess confused or blurred sexual identity, rather than trying to convince them they are straight. Colin told us he tried to address his conflicting homosexual feelings with three different therapists; because Colin was a father, all of them denied the possibility of his being homosexual. As a result of having his reality invalidated, Colin further buried his feelings and did not deal with them until twenty years later:

> Last week I passed by a construction site, and a man was pouring concrete. He had a beautiful body. He had on nothing but jeans and shoes; that was it. I had this strong sexual feeling toward him. I have had those feelings consistently in my life, but I had not looked at them very seriously. But I've wondered what they meant. I've worried about these feelings, but was afraid to talk about them. I tried three times in therapy to talk about my homosexual feelings. The male therapist I was with each time said, "You're not homosexual." I don't know if they were saying that because they were afraid to talk about it or not. But as each of them said that to me, there was a part of me that wanted to hear it, and I felt a sense of relief, even though I didn't really believe it. Now, twenty years later, I cannot push the feelings aside any longer. In the past I would bring up my homosexuality in therapy

because it felt like something that wouldn't go away. But I'm not sure
I brought it up with any intention of acting on it. So I have been afraid
of these feelings, and that's what stopped me from doing anything
about them. But I have also let that fear dominate me because I was
committed to providing this model of a family. Just admiring that
man's body without any shame was such a wonderful thing for me.

Miller (1979a) also reported that a few of the men he interviewed were concerned enough about their homosexual feelings to
seek counseling before entering a marital relationship. In each case
the man was led to believe that a heterosexual marriage and parenthood would "cure all his ills." In fact, when one of the men fathered a child premaritally, the psychiatrist underscored this as proof
that the man was "genuinely heterosexual." A second respondent
told of his eagerness to accept his counselor's assessments: "The
shrink told me what I was dying to hear: 'A person as nice as you
couldn't be homosexual.' What he should have done was get me to
accept my homosexual self rather than some imaginary heterosexual self. But I believed him because I desperately wanted a home
and someone to love to come home to" (quoted in Miller, 1979a,
p. 546).

Become an Activist

Opportunities for activism on behalf of gay fathers abound (Barret,
1998). Simply having gay-positive books on your professional book-
shelf sends a message to all that you may know something about
sexual orientation and that you are ready to discuss it. Even placing gay magazines such as the *Advocate* or *Out* in your waiting room
allows all clients to learn about sexual minorities. Investigating the
laws about adoption in your state and becoming an advocate for gay
and lesbian adoption can be enormously helpful. Asking school personnel how they interact with gay fathers and offering to do a work-
shop for teachers will help the children of gay parents have a more
positive school experience. Contacting your local gay parenting

group and asking to meet with some gay fathers who will educate you about their lives is another activity that will pay off.

The time has come to see the gay rights movement in the context of the larger human rights movement that liberates all people. Refuting the myths about homosexuality in both professional and personal discussions is a task that awaits all of us. The power of this opportunity is evident in the comments of one gay father:

> While on an airplane, I was seated next to a man who began our conversation by raging against diversity training in the workplace. Later he talked about his kids and then asked if I were married and had children. I took a deep breath and said, "I'm gay, and I've adopted two kids." At first I thought he was going to attack me. But as we talked more and more he became very interested and asked great questions. As we walked off the plane together he said to me, "Thanks for taking such a risk. I have never talked to a gay person before, and I learned a lot from you. I now see this issue is different from what I had thought." Obviously he had never been challenged in a way that would allow him to examine his prejudices.

3

The Many Faces of Gay Fatherhood

Gil of San Antonio has two sons whose parents are from different cultures. Their mother is Hispanic, and their father is from a South Pacific island culture. Both of these cultures have very negative views of gay men and lesbians. Gil and his partner coparent along with his former wife and her current husband.

Since I came out to my family and friends about four years ago, life as a gay father of two teenage boys has been the happiest and most rewarding time of my life. When my wife and I split, we initially told the boys that the separation and later the divorce was primarily due to their parents not being able to live together happily. Thankfully, since this was a truth they had witnessed, they accepted this reason without questioning us further. As I began to build a new life, I promised myself I would no longer shelter myself or my loved ones from my personal truths. So I was open to myself, and in my apartment I did not hide gay-themed books and movies from my sons. One spring day I decided to "test the waters" and asked my sons what they thought about homosexuality. They were raised to be open-minded, and they responded in an understanding and open way. I came to appreciate their openness in a new way.

I went through the usual coming-out process and had my share of the dating scene. Being thirty-five, I was ready for the freedom and consequences of being single and gay. I went out with several guys, but nothing serious developed until I met Phil. He lived on the East Coast, and we met at a professional conference. Since I was in San Antonio, we "dated" electronically until we had the chance for a long visit. After several months and spending more time together, we decided ours was a permanent relationship, and Phil moved in with me. This was going to be the first time the boys were going to see me with another man. Of course, at first, I was extremely nervous but soon I realized the more I was myself, the easier the boys could accept Phil and a new version of their dad. Over time they have come to love Phil, and he gets along with them so well! Today they have their own relationship, and I am grateful when I see them talking to him or making plans to spend time together. My youngest son refers to us as "the dads." We are all together at least every other weekend and on most school holidays. Our life seems so normal, and, naturally, I have to stop myself from being a drama queen by making comments on what is happening. I don't want to spoil the happiness we share. I am also very grateful that my former wife and her new husband accept Phil and our relationship.

Phil, the boys, and I go everywhere together and don't consider ourselves different or exceptional. We are a family and act just like all families. We laugh, become frustrated, talk, and cry just like other families. We attend Catholic mass every Sunday and are accepted by our pastor. We get involved in our community and enjoy just about every activity we explore. We don't consider ourselves different, and I don't think we act differently than other families. Thankfully there has not been a single incident that would remind us that others are uncomfortable with us.

Being a father is easily the most important role in my life. I love my sons, and I love being their dad. They make my life easy. But, still, I can't help worrying about how my being gay is for them. I feel very confident confronting homophobia and feel very confident and comfortable with who I am. However, the father in me wants very much to protect my sons from being hurt because others have negative feelings about gay people. Ben tells me that in high school the worst name you can call someone is "gay." Times sure haven't changed much from when I was in high school twenty years ago. Kids can be so vicious with one another, and I would hate to see my sons suffer because of me. One weekend my younger son, Sam, asked if he could have a friend come over to play for the day. I didn't have any problem with his request and said OK. As we picked up his friend, Tim, I spoke with his parents. The boys had a great time, and when we dropped Tim off at the end of the day, Sam and I had a long talk. I asked him what he would do and how he might feel if Tim's parents would say Tim could not play with him anymore because of me, and how he would feel if Tim told everyone at school that his father is gay, or what might happen if Tim told him he did not want to be friends any longer because he did not like gay people. Although we talked about these possible scenarios in detail, I still worry. Sam seems to understand what he would need to do to protect himself if he is faced with negative comments because of me, but I just can't let go of my need to protect him. One of the things that is unique about gay and lesbian parents is the threat of ridicule. I don't think this will ever end, and I want my sons to be prepared. Just like it is for me, Sam and Ben will have to keep on coming out about their dad. I no longer feel guilty about this. They know I will be there for them just as they have constantly supported me. Our lives are paralleled and linked, and I know that I can model ways to handle difficult situations for them.

I used to think that I would never come out of the closet. I did not want to hurt my kids, and that kept me confused for a long time. Today I know that they learn a lot from my being gay. Being gay can be a liability, but it also can be an enriching experience. And that's exactly what I think Phil and I do for the boys.

Gil

San Antonio, Texas

TYPES OF GAY FATHERING

As you can already tell, every gay father's experience is different. Some men, like Gil, marry and remain married, playing an important role in the rearing of their offspring before they finally decide to leave. In many cases spouses do not know of their husband's homosexuality. In others, the wives know and tolerate their husband's lifestyle. Other wives participate in joint custody arrangements with their husbands, despite knowledge of their spouse's homosexuality. Gil is an example of a man who lived with his wife and sons and who was able to leave and start a new life with his wife's support. Some gay fathers never marry the mother of their children. Even fewer rear their youngsters alone as single fathers, because custody rulings in favor of gay men are rare, just as they are for single fathers.

Until now we have discussed the common experiences of gay fathers in order to draw a general profile. Despite these common experiences, each case has its individual characteristics and complications that require different approaches. Becoming aware of the varied gay father family configurations will enrich your skills in working with gay families. In this chapter we will draw a profile of gay father family types from the research literature and from our own case studies.

DEMOGRAPHIC INFORMATION

It is impossible to give exact figures on the numbers of gay fathers in the United States. It is difficult to project the numbers of homosexual men, much less the numbers of gay fathers who live under a double risk of disclosing their sexual orientation. Recall from Chapter One that there is debate about the percentage of men who are gay and that most experts now believe the figure is approximately 5 percent. Statistics also suggest that 10 percent of all clients of mental health agencies are gay or lesbian (Woodman & Lenna, 1980). Estimates are only best guesses, and the numbers cited (although dated) may be valid today. Of the homosexual population, projected numbers of heterosexually married gay men are approximately 20 percent (Harry, 1983). Of these marriages, approximately half result in children (Bell & Weinberg, 1978). Altogether, estimates are that as many as two million gay fathers live in the United States and Canada today (Bozett, 1984b).

In the samples that have been studied, most of the men live separately from their spouses and see their children only periodically. Bozett (1980) reported that seventeen of the eighteen men (94 percent) he studied lived apart from their wives; Miller (1979a) found that twenty-three of the forty men (58 percent) he interviewed lived apart from their wives; and Skeen and Robinson (1984) reported that twenty-two of the thirty men (73 percent) in their study were separated or divorced from their wives. Recall the discussion of custody issues in Chapter One. For legal reasons many divorced gay fathers try to keep their sexual orientation out of court proceedings. It is safe to assume that the number of gay fathers may be higher than studies suggest.

GAY FATHER FAMILY CONFIGURATIONS

Being a parent is difficult enough, and research shows that being an unwed, adoptive, step, or single parent further complicates the role. Layer any one of these roles with one or both parents being gay, and you have a set of highly complex circumstances. The stress level for gay father families is extraordinary, and each family configuration has its own inherent problems. Few treatment models exist. Work with gay father families demands compassion and creativity. Openness and flexibility are cornerstones of successful practice. The first step in intervention is for you to identify the family configuration of the gay father with whom you are working. Having identified the family type, you are able to pinpoint unique problems, which you can then match to unique solutions. Figure 3.1 shows the eight types of gay father family configurations. One could hypothesize that the more squiggly and broken lines there are in a family unit, the more inherent problems contained in that family configuration.

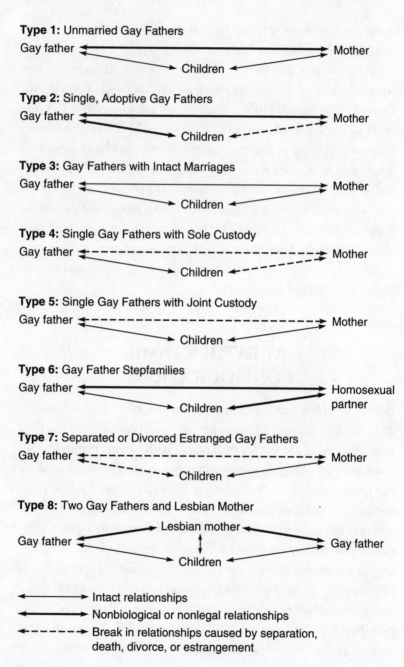

Type 1: Unmarried Gay Fathers

Gay father ⟷ Mother
Children

Type 2: Single, Adoptive Gay Fathers

Gay father ⟷ Mother
Children

Type 3: Gay Fathers with Intact Marriages

Gay father ⟷ Mother
Children

Type 4: Single Gay Fathers with Sole Custody

Gay father ⟷ Mother
Children

Type 5: Single Gay Fathers with Joint Custody

Gay father ⟷ Mother
Children

Type 6: Gay Father Stepfamilies

Gay father ⟷ Homosexual partner
Children

Type 7: Separated or Divorced Estranged Gay Fathers

Gay father ⟷ Mother
Children

Type 8: Two Gay Fathers and Lesbian Mother

Lesbian mother
Gay father ⟷ ⟷ Gay father
Children

⟷ Intact relationships
⟷ Nonbiological or nonlegal relationships
⟷ - - - - Break in relationships caused by separation, death, divorce, or estrangement

Figure 3.1. Gay Father Family Configurations

TYPE 1: UNMARRIED
GAY FATHERS

The Type 1 family includes an unmarried gay man and woman with one or more children. This family configuration can evolve for many different reasons, each of which carries its own unique problems. The man and woman may be genuinely in love, and the pregnancy could be unplanned. The mother may or may not know of the father's sexual orientation. If you are a practitioner involved with this kind of family, you are likely to encounter many of the same problems you might find with unplanned pregnancies and unwed parents, coupled with the factor of the father's homosexuality. Some challenging questions, for example, might be: Should the couple marry, given the father's sexual orientation? and if so, What kinds of problems and possible solutions in such marriages can be foreseen by both sides?

The father and mother may not be in love, and neither party may desire to marry. Discussions about custody arrangements must include the mother's knowledge of the father's homosexuality. Some Type 1 families include preplanned pregnancies by gay men and lesbian women. These arrangements are often loosely thought out as a means for homosexual men and women to have children of their own. In some instances, the gay father and lesbian mother genuinely love one another and wish to live together, either married or unmarried. In others, the mother is artificially inseminated with the gay man's sperm. You must facilitate issues around parental responsibilities, having outside sexual partners, children's exposure to sexual partners, what to tell the children, what names to give parents' intimate partners, and how to define these intimate partners within the family. More commonly, however, you deal with helping gay men and lesbian women work out a mutual, often not legally binding, custody arrangement so that both parents can share equally in the child's upbringing, in keeping with the original plan.

TYPE 2: SINGLE, ADOPTIVE
GAY FATHERS

In 1980, there were approximately fifty-two thousand never-married single adoptive fathers. The percentage of that number that are gay is unknown. Adoptions by heterosexual single men are very difficult because practitioners and society do not approve of single men rearing children. A man parenting a child without a wife who can provide nurturing is somehow seen as unnatural. Never-married gay men who want to adopt are especially closely scrutinized, and their sexual orientation becomes a pressing concern. Gay men who are fortunate enough to become single adoptive fathers have limited choices of school-age boys who have mental or physical disabilities or who are members of a minority race, delinquent, or otherwise "hard to place." Single gay foster fathers also fall into the Type 2 family category.

Becoming a father through adoption can bring up many issues. If the agency does not ask, is it expected that the gay father will reveal his sexual orientation? If he does take that step, what might the consequences be? How does "passing" as straight affect the father's self-esteem? Jeremy had this to say about his decision not to tell: "I had to weigh which desire was stronger—to be true to myself, my community, and my friends, or to become a parent. . . . I decided not to offer information that I am gay. . . . I didn't feel that it was relevant to whether I should be a parent or not. No one ever asked specifically, but still, not saying anything was an issue for me" (quoted in Drucker, 1998, p. 162).

As a practitioner, you will work to help these fathers face the usual challenge of rearing a child alone without societal support and in spite of societal disapproval. You and your client may also have to address the added dimension of his being a white father with a black child or the challenge of rearing a child with a disability or one who acts out. You can combine clinical skills from two distinct areas: working with adoptive parents and working with parents with difficult children. You can modify the merging of these skills to include special problems that relate to the father's homosexuality. Almost always this involves assisting the father in disclosing to a child who already has significant problems, asking him or her to accept yet another huge problem. Faced with rejection, these fathers do not ha e the biological ties that sometimes guarantee a parent-child bond. The "blood is thicker than water" rule does not hold in the case of the single adoptive father. Surprisingly, though, these children's past history in dealing with life's problems often sensitizes them to understand and accept their adoptive father's homosexuality.

TYPE 3: GAY FATHERS WITH INTACT MARRIAGES

The Type 3 family comprises a gay father living with his spouse in an intact marriage with one or more children. The spouse may or may not know of her husband's homosexuality. In cases where the wife is not aware of her husband's sexual orientation, you work predominately with the father around issues of disclosure or nondisclosure to the spouse. With increasing numbers of married women being infected with HIV from bisexual or homosexual husbands, health risks and the mother's rights raise ethical issues in regard to disclosure that the gay father must resolve. Fathers need support in disclosing their sexual orientation to their spouses and in working out an equitable arrangement between them. In a minority of instances, you find a wife who is willing to live with her husband knowing of his sexual activity. Today that arrangement is less common because of the risk of HIV, because fewer women are willing to deny themselves a life of their own, and because fewer gay men are willing to stifle their true selves.

In cases in which fathers have already told their wives, you need to work with both parents around establishing an agreeable arrangement. In some situations, that arrangement involves separation and divorce. When it does, you are confronted with the same issues of divorce, single parenting, and custody arrangements that occur in heterosexual marriages, layered with the complication of the father's sexual orientation.

In some Type 3 families the fathers have male partners. You will find that in these circumstances, including all three adults in counseling helps in resolving conflicts. Situations in which all parties can openly communicate their feelings, show empathy and compassion, and develop amicable and cooperative relationships benefit the children and help them adjust to the new family arrangement.

TYPE 4: SINGLE GAY FATHERS WITH SOLE CUSTODY

The Type 4 family is one in which the gay father has sole custody of his children due to separation, divorce, or the death of his spouse. This family configuration usually occurs as a result of spousal death or the mother's voluntarily giving the father full custody. Recall in Chapter One the legal difficulties that single gay fathers face as they attempt to gain sole custody of their children.

You must help your client handle all the issues and concerns of being a single parent as well as those associated with being in a double minority, male and gay. Single parenting brings enormous amounts of stress for men and women, but the role is further exaggerated when men must struggle to find a balance between their roles as a single male parent and as a single gay man (see, for example, Robinson & Barret, 1986). Only about 10 percent of single parents are custodial single fathers. The additional burden of rearing children as a homosexual father may raise the level of stress to unbearable heights. Stress reduction counseling, therefore, is a chief goal for this family type. The issue of disclosure may or may not be relevant, depending on the age of the children and the father's lifestyle. For men who want to live openly as gay, a goal is to help them reconcile their lifestyle with that of rearing children in a healthy environment and dealing with society's stereotypes. The gay father in this family must face society's wrath more than fathers in many other family configurations, because there is no female directly involved. The Freudian belief of maternal deprivation applied together with the myths of gay fathering makes this father especially vulnerable to attack.

TYPE 5: SINGLE GAY FATHERS WITH JOINT CUSTODY

The Type 5 family is one in which the father is separated or divorced and shares joint custody with his wife. In some instances the gay father has not disclosed his homosexuality to his spouse, so his sexuality is not an issue in the custody decision. Although he has legal custody rights, he conceals his homosexuality and lifestyle for fear of losing parental rights. Because custody decisions rarely allow openly gay fathers any rights, Type 5 arrangements are usually worked out between the husband and wife, as the following example illustrates:

Being a gay father who has chosen to share parenting on an equal basis with my former wife seems to many people a contradiction in lifestyles. It certainly has proved to be complicated. For me, claiming an ongoing role in the parenting process was a logical step. Accepting my sexual orientation and my desire to share life with another man meant that marriage must end. Both my wife and I had made a conscious decision that each of us wanted to be a parent. From the day she and my son came home from the hospital, both of us shared the joys and responsibilities of parenting. We consciously avoided what we felt to be the stereotypical parenting roles prevalent in 1973, the year our son was born. When our marriage ended four years later, it was unthinkable to me that I would give up my parenting role.

> Fortunately, my wife wanted us to continue to share the raising of our
> son, so we had no legal problems in establishing joint custody on an
> alternate-week basis.

You must assist parents in making decisions regarding custody and visitation rights. Complex issues exist regarding consistency in discipline from one household to another and how to handle arrangements when the mother has a boyfriend who may be hostile toward homosexuality. Or, if the gay father dates occasionally, the mother may have concerns over having her child exposed to intimacy between two men. The stepfather may resent having the child spend weeks in his house after having been "contaminated in a house full of homosexuals." Again, the kinds of issues that any family would have to address when making joint custody decisions are confounded by issues of sexual orientation.

TYPE 6: GAY FATHER STEPFAMILIES

The Type 6 family is more complicated than Type 5 because the father has a live-in male partner who essentially becomes a stepparent to the child. Many gay partners do not find such a relationship appealing, because they must share the partner in a complexity of relationships with children, ex-spouse, and possibly her new boyfriend or husband. Heterosexual stepfamilies are by nature very complex. Problems interfere with family harmony: "A host of extra people and pressures push and tug at the step family, making the determination of its own destiny difficult" (Einstein, 1982, p. 7). The issue of homosexuality adds new dimensions to the problems that all such families must address. Children can become confused by and jealous of their father's love interest. The father's partner must confront many of the same issues as that of any stepparent, plus additional hostility because he is a gay man in the position of parenting someone else's child. Often he has entered into a family in which the gay father and his children have had a lifetime to establish their relationships. The father's partner is an outsider in many ways and may find himself having to create instant, intimate relationships with children he barely knows. They may be virtual strangers and resent each other from time to time. The mother is often suspicious of the father's male partner and may worry about the safety of her children from sexual molestation as well as the development of her children's gender identity in the company of two intimate men.

You can effectively work with this family type by using the model of stepfamily dynamics. Disciplining children, household rules, division of household labor, family members seeing each other undressed, sexual matters, jealousy, amount of time and attention the father distributes between his children and male partner, and parent-stepparent-child relationships are just some of the problems that all stepfamilies must face. It is important that you treat the gay stepfamily as a family unit with many of the same problems as heterosexual families, rather than as a group of unrelated individuals sharing a residence (Baptiste, 1987).

As one might guess, the ideal way for families to avoid problems is for the members to seek counseling before engaging in this type of family arrangement. But you will not always have the luxury of seeing gay stepfamilies before they have set up housekeeping. The usual custom is for families to seek counseling only after problems have begun to surface. To work through problems inherent in this family type, it is crucial to include in counseling the father, his partner, the mother, her boyfriend or husband, and the children when they are at an appropriate age to benefit from inclusion. Because there are few guidelines for being a gay father with a male partner who functions as a stepparent, men in this role, along with other family members, must create their rules based on individual personalities, living arrangements, and the ages and sexes of the children. Therapists agree that cooperation and unity between the biological parents is a key to minimizing conflict in stepfamilies (Visher & Visher, 1978).

TYPE 7: SEPARATED OR DIVORCED ESTRANGED GAY FATHERS

This family type is one of estrangement, in which the ex-wife refuses all contact with the gay father. The children are too young to make up their own minds, or they are prevented by the courts or the mother from seeing the father. Some children who are old enough to make their own decisions reject their fathers.

The Type 7 father has little or no contact with his family, primarily due to his family's inability or refusal to understand and accept his sexual preference. Your clinical goals are obviously limited by this family configuration. You can focus counseling concerns around the father's feelings of rejection, alienation, isolation, and bitterness. Helping these men reach out to other fathers in similar situations can enable them to get the support they need to ease their isolation. Sessions on self-worth and self-acceptance can also help combat their feelings of rejection.

TYPE 8: TWO GAY FATHERS AND LESBIAN MOTHER

A more atypical arrangement is one in which a lesbian woman agrees to be artificially inseminated with the mixed sperm from two gay men. This practice, usually found in larger metropolitan areas with heavy concentrations of gay men and lesbian women, results in children who are reared by three parents. Most of these parental threesomes do not cohabit as a family unit, although some do: "As an adult, I chose to have a child and to share that responsibility with the two gay men who are my closest friends. The four of us (Bert, Geof, daughter Veronica, and I) live together as a family unit and are accepted by our friends and families. . . . I quickly learned to recognize my situation for what it is: a small minority within a minority group" (Schulenburg, 1985, p. 4).

Type 8 families could be a subcategory of Type 1, except for the fact that there are three parents who often live together. Although you must deal with many of the same issues that come up in your work with Type 1 families, additional unresolved questions emerge in the Type 8 family: How do three parents maintain consistency in child rearing when it is hard enough for two to maintain such consistency? How do you explain to the kids that they have three parents instead of two? And as he or she gets older, how does the child explain his or her situation to the heterosexual world? An even further reaching question is, What happens if the three-parent family splits up and each parent goes his or her separate way? What are the custody arrangements and financial implications for such a complicated state of affairs? As you can imagine, there are no pat answers for these types of experimental family arrangements. The nature of this family configuration demands creative problem solving, open dialogue among all involved parties, and frequently an objective ear to assist the family in resolving these issues.

Gay Parents Among the Caseload: One Practitioner's Experiences

I have worked with three cases involving gay parents. I had my first case when I worked in a psychiatric hospital on the adolescent unit. The daughter of a gay father came into the hospital. The fourteen-year-old, who entered the hospital for chemical dependency and conduct disorder, was in the custody of her mother. There was a lot of tension with the staff and family because Dad was gay and living with his partner. The staff, mostly registered nurses and counselors, had a lot of difficulty adjusting to the fact that the girl's father was gay. Negative comments were made such as, "This is unheard of, a gay father!" or "How dare he have this child in his home with his lover living there!" The staff tossed around terms like "fag" and "queer" in the hallways to refer to the girl's father. They saw Mom as the one who was trying hard and doing all the work, and the father, although he paid all the hospital bills, as not caring about what was going on. Under the circumstances, I felt that the father was giving as much support as he could, given the fact that he lived sixty miles away. The father's homosexuality overshadowed the real, more crucial problems in the case because it went against the staff's Southern Baptist values. Their judgmental nature interfered with the helping process for the daughter. They were unprofessional in expressing biases within earshot of other patients when their comments should have been confined to the staff areas.

They were making the fact that this child had a gay father *the* problem. But there was a lot more going on than just the fact that the girl had a gay father and that there was a divorce in the family. There were a lot of interpersonal problems and peer pressure that had brought her into the substance abuse world. The biggest problems were the child's chemical dependency and feelings of depression and poor self-esteem. There were a lot of typical adolescent problems that were compounded by her drug use. The child was blatantly defiant and didn't listen to her mother.

Practitioners need to keep an open mind that there are many ways of life that they might not have grown up with. In cases such as this, staff must be more understanding of what is going on and that this is the person's chosen way to live. We must be continually aware that what's OK for this person may not be OK for us, but in that person's situation it's perfectly fine and acceptable. That's the way those clients are coping with life. If they're not having any major problems with their lifestyles, leave well enough alone. If practitioners can't handle the case, they should refer the client to someone else who they feel can better handle the case. In my own cases, I put aside whatever prejudices I have until I've read and researched the special population I'm working with. A female social worker who had the case before me couldn't wait to get rid of the case. She was happier to get rid of this case than any other she ever gave me. It stemmed from her own discomfort, lack of knowledge, and inexperience in dealing with a gay parent.

It is important that practitioners approach gay father families in the same way that they would a heterosexual couple. When a lover is involved, that is basically a stepfamily relationship. The wrinkle in it is that Dad is living with another man and they are partners. Being gay is not the issue. The issue is dealing with the family unit as a whole. Practitioners must alter their view to accommodate the fact that Dad is living with his lover. If it's a good relationship, don't mess with it. Leave well enough alone. What practitioners must consider is the daughter's view of what is going on and whether or not she's comfortable with it. That is an issue for individual therapy. If Dad and his partner are comfortable and the daughter is having problems accepting their homosexuality, that's the daughter's problem and should be dealt with in individual therapy with her. If the child is having problems with Dad's companion, that's more of a family issue, and I would treat that as I would the "wicked stepmom" problem and involve the whole family. The same goes if the "stepdad" tries to discipline the child. If it's a family problem, view it as a family problem. If it's an individual's problem, deal with it on an individual basis. But if it's not broken, don't fix it. Approach the family with a gay parent like any other family, and if the gay issue becomes a problem, deal with it in perspective as you would any other secondary problem.

Another case was a child who had returned a second time. Her mother was a lesbian with a girlfriend, and there were a lot of domestic problems. Although the child seemed to handle her mother's homosexuality, she didn't like the lover telling her what to do. There were several episodes when they would have knock-down, drag-out fights. The child wanted one person to discipline her. Discipline tended to be violent. The child would pull a knife or make homicidal threats to the girlfriend. With the exception of physical violence, the underlying conflict was the same as that found in any stepfamily. We had to educate the parents about what is acceptable discipline and what is borderline child abuse. Our goal was to get the child to handle her frustrations and her feelings about the real issue, which was her dysfunctional behavior in school. We tried to get her to sit through the day without blowing up at the teacher who was telling her what to do. There was a lot of family strife, and lesbian parents weren't looked upon favorably by the extended family. The staff also had a hard time accepting their lifestyle, although it was more acceptable than the gay father family. The male staff felt more uncomfortable than the female staff.

The core issue of getting the child back into the home and dealing with the family problems was hurt by the negative comments that were made about the homosexuality. The family clashed with what the staff felt a family should be, and they were really uncomfortable with it. They viewed homosexuality as a sin and believed the clients would burn in hell for the way they were living. It was difficult for them to feel comfortable with this child's mother coming in or the mother's girlfriend coming to pick up the child. A lot of people questioned how legal it was for the lover to sign the child out on a pass. But it was just like a stepmom instead of a stepdad.

The third case was a lesbian mother who was physically abusive to her child. The child was removed from the home. Mom had a lover who also had a child that was getting most of the attention in the home. The physical abuse, though, was the key issue. Our goal was to get Mom involved with the child through family counseling and to be understanding of the daughter. Mom had a very black-and-white view of the world and an attitude of "How dare you people tell me how to raise my child." She wasn't happy with the Department of Social Services (DSS) nosing in her life. She was upset with their obtrusive home visits that scrutinized her every move.

Once I acknowledged the fact that the parents were gay, there were certain issues that were different. The facts that DSS was involved and that "my lifestyle is not acceptable" had to be dealt with. At some level the facts had to be acknowledged and determined whether they were an issue or not. In the last case I described, the daughter never mentioned her mother's lesbianism as a problem in the family counseling sessions. But in the individual sessions, the daughter revealed that she had a difficult time accepting the fact that her mother was in the next room sleeping with another woman. At thirteen, the daughter was concerned that she too might turn out to be a lesbian. She was just hitting adolescence and struggling with her own sexual identity and her relationship with boys. Mom's biggest concern was that when a relationship with a previous lover broke up, her daughter would still hold an emotional attachment to her mother's former sexual partner. Mom would say, "That relationship is over and done with! Why do you keep dredging up the past?" The daughter had really bonded to one of her mother's former girlfriends, and this was causing some difficulty in the relationship. The daughter wanted to go see this woman, but Mom's view was that the girlfriend was out of her life and therefore out of the daughter's life.

TIPS FOR PRACTITIONERS

One major challenge for practitioners is to be aware of the confusion and guilt that often accompany a homosexual identity within a heterosexual family setting. As we pointed out, the coming-out process for gay fathers can be lengthy and painful. Your major goals as a practitioner include putting the father's sexuality in perspective, fostering self-acceptance, providing network opportunities, and identifying gay father family types.

Put the Father's Sexuality in Perspective

Your experience with gay fathers might occur indirectly through the primary treatment of a child or spouse. When a child or spouse is the primary client and the father has not come for treatment, you must be careful not to get sidetracked into focusing on the father's sexual orientation as the central issue, as doing so only directs attention away from pertinent treatment concerns. You must place the parent's sexual orientation in perspective and not address it as the problem, as is often the tendency. Instead, you can address the gay father's sexuality as a separate issue if, in fact, a family member is having difficulty about the homosexuality. Otherwise, you foster treatment most by focusing on the relevant problems and putting the parent's homosexuality in context.

Work with the Family System When Appropriate

Helping gay fathers may also mean helping the nuclear and extended family resolve their issues related to his sexual orientation. You will find that working with the entire family system, composed of gay fathers and their wives and children, can also be useful in conflict resolution. Referrals to the local gay fathers support groups are another way to achieve this end. Although not the norm, some couples successfully integrate ex-spouses into their support system and often plan family meetings that include all involved parties when important decisions must be made. As spouses make decisions about custody issues and participation at family celebrations, you may need to include the ex-spouse, children, parents, brothers, and sisters in counseling sessions. Occasionally, you will be called on to work with fathers and their male partners (and sometimes wives) to help them work through the family transformation. The family as a whole generally is involved in a crisis and may need assistance as they move through the process of integrating the father's newly discovered sexual orientation. One gay father reported that he was elated that his children and ex-wife would be living adjacent to him and his lover, enabling them all to parent the children. Such mutual respect is a source of strength for children. Other parenting issues when a partner is present may include the role of the "stepfather" as well as possibly integrating families formed by two gay fathers and their children.

Identify Gay Father Configurations

You can most effectively treat gay father families when you understand that there are many diverse types of gay father families, each type requiring different intervention approaches. Identifying the type of family configuration is important in order to match appropriate treatment goals. Once you have identified the configuration, you will find that a marriage and family therapy orientation similar to that used with heterosexual families works best. Drawing from your work with unwed and unplanned pregnancies, adoption, single parenting, and stepfamilies, you can strengthen your approach by modifying conventional marriage and family therapy techniques to include the added dimension of homosexuality. As we have already mentioned, the most important point is that you should treat gay father families as a family unit, as you would a heterosexual family, rather than as a collection of unrelated individuals living together. Important counseling goals are to help family members clarify relationships, clarify and understand their own behaviors and interactions, and improve communication capitalizing on the special nature of the relationships as when children may have the advantage of parenting from several "parents," all of whom love them (Baptiste, 1987). As we have already said, prior experience in working with unwed parents, adoptive and single parents, and stepparents provides many of the clinical skills you need to address unique therapeutic issues of gay father families.

4

Children of Gay Fathers

Ben lives with his mom and her husband most of the week and spends weekends with his dad (Gil, whose story opened Chapter Three) and his partner. A typical high school student, Ben fills his days with academics and music and sports. He writes about his experience of having a gay father and parents who have divorced.

My parents were married about a year before I was born and continued to be married until I was twelve and in middle school. When they divorced they would not tell me all of the reasons. At the time, I probably would not have understood anyway, since I had no experience or contact with homosexuality. About all I knew then I had learned from reading. After the divorce I lived with my mom in our old house, and my dad moved to an apartment a few miles away. We spent the weekdays with Mom and went to Dad's every weekend. My parents got along during that time, but I was struggling. As a matter of fact, those were the most difficult years I had ever faced. About a year after the divorce, Mom started dating. That same year I got into a lot of trouble, purely juvenile stuff, causing a lot of tension between Dad and me, and Mom and me, and eventually between Mom and Dad. Things got so bad and the situation got so stressed, until they came to a head over spring break in 1997. As each of us expressed our anger, lots of secrets were revealed, strong emotions were expressed, and no one really was able to listen. We just attacked each other. To me it was like a war where alliances changed like the seasonal wind, and finally things became so hurtful that I just clammed up for fear that whatever I said was going to be turned against me.

This tension was mostly between my Dad and me. My little brother, Sam, seemed to be on Dad's side one minute and mine the next. He sure got along with Dad better than I did. After that week we moved into a new home, since Mom and her boyfriend had decided to get married. Gradually things began to calm down. Mom and her boyfriend did get married, a second marriage for both of them, and I inherited a new stepbrother, which has been a source of both strife and learning.

Back then I could truly call myself ignorant when it came to understanding homosexuality. Because of the way I had been raised, my views were mostly negative. From school and from TV I had learned that "gay" was not a good thing. Students at school used the term "gay" as a way to say the other was stupid, only the insult was way more degrading. To call someone or something "gay" was like saying they or it was so dumb that it did not deserve recognition. After discovering my Dad is gay, I began to see that gays were not aliens; instead, most of them were normal, just like my dad. Even though the idea of homosexuality is a turn-off for me, I can understand that people who have a same-sex attraction do not deserve to be hated just because of that. I truly feel that everything that has happened to me has been for the best. Since my parents split up and my dad came out, my eyes have been opened to a wonderful world where people are seen as a duality in the most basic way.

I have never had anyone know about my dad, except a few carefully selected friends who I know would not tell anyone. I'd like to think that I am prepared if someone teases me about Dad. The most mature and correct way to deal with it would be to simply state that it is none of their business and that someone's sexual life is off-limits. I know how mean some kids can be, and I also know that some will not stop until you threaten to fight. Some kids only understand violence. I doubt I would retaliate physically unless I feel like I am in real danger.

Having a gay dad is just like having a normal dad, though in some ways I think it is better. My dad knows about growth and understands the need for self-expression. Still, he can be firm, just, and reliable. Of course, those are qualities my dad has just because of the person he is. Gay dads tend to understand and empathize with their children better. I keep in mind that everything is relative. Not all gay dads are understanding and not all straight dads have empathy. I try to remember that humans can never be labeled accurately. Being gay or straight, rich or poor, black or white isn't a reflection of everything about a person. The only thing labels like these tell you is that the person is either gay or straight, rich or poor, black or white, and nothing else can accurately be assumed. My dad is a great guy, and I am happy to call him Dad.

Ben

San Antonio, Texas

HAVING A GAY FATHER

Often the children of gay fathers are seen as innocent victims. But such an attitude is simply one more example of gay-negativity. The children of gay fathers are like all children: those who have fathers who love them and create close relationships with them seem to get along just fine. Those with fathers who are distant or rejecting or who suffer from other psychological problems are likely to develop problems as well. As Ben talked with us, he covered most of the issues relevant to children of gay fathers. Some of the myths discussed in Chapter Two are applied with most vehemence in discussions about children. People typically express concerns about the likelihood that children raised in gay families will become homosexual themselves or that the gay parent will attempt to seduce the same-sex child. As we already have stated, research indicates that both of these myths are simply not supported in actual life. Children in gay families are as well adjusted as all kids (Golombok & Tasker,

1994). They excel in school, sports, and other extracurricular activities, and they have drug and alcohol problems, get pregnant, and don't apply themselves in schoolwork—just like all young people. In short, there are no indications that having a gay father is inherently an impairment in child development (McIntyre, 1994).

The notion that gay men as fathers will sexually molest their children is one of the most frequently cited rationales for denying custody (Patterson, 1992). In recent years, research on incest and family violence has brought renewed attention to this topic. Yet studies on incest involving homosexuals rarely appear in the literature; this may be a reflection of the few gay men who participate in incest or a reflection of the strong taboo against talking about such sexual contacts. As we stated earlier, child molesters who are incest perpetrators are generally heterosexual men (Jones & McFarlane, 1980). Gay parents and their partners are involved in virtually no cases of child sexual abuse (DeFrancis, 1976; Gebhard, Gagnon, Pomeroy, & Christenson, 1965; Geiser, 1979; Richardson, 1981).

Jenny and her associates (1994) found that of 269 children treated for sexual abuse at a large urban hospital over a one-year time period, only two of the adult perpetrators could be identified as gay or lesbian. Their study showed that approximately 75 percent of child sexual abuse was perpetrated by the adult heterosexual male spouse or boyfriend of a family member. As the statistics now stand, it appears that children living with gay parents are at less risk of sexual abuse than children with heterosexual parents (Jenny, Roesler, & Poyer, 1994).

"CATCHING" HOMOSEXUALITY

Some people fear that children living in gay households will "catch" homosexuality from their parent (the germ theory of homosexuality). Others worry that these children have a congenital predisposition toward homosexuality that would be effectively curbed by placing them in heterosexual environments (Miller, 1979a). Basing their position in part on psychoanalytic and social learning theories that emphasize the major role of the same-sex and opposite-sex parent in psychosexual development, proponents of this position ignore both the heterosexuality of children raised in single-parent households and the homosexuality of children raised by two heterosexual parents. Research does not support either the germ theory or the congenital predisposition view (Bozett, 1980, 1982, 1987, 1989; Green, 1978; Miller, 1979a). Although most of the studies on "catching" homosexuality involve lesbians as subjects, the consensus does not support the contention that homosexuality is transmitted from lesbian mothers or from gay fathers to their children (Pennington, 1987; Steckel, 1987).

In the most comprehensive recent study about the sexual orientation of the children of gay parents, Bailey, Bobrow, Wolfe, and Mikach (1995) received questionnaires from eighty-two sons of fifty-five gay fathers. Of the seventy-five sons whose sexual orientation could be rated reliably, sixty-eight were heterosexual, indicating that only 9 percent were either gay or bisexual. Another interesting finding in this study is that the sexual orientation of these sons was not related to the number of years spent living in the gay father's homes, nor to the frequency of current contact with the gay father, nor to the quality of the relationship they shared. As a matter of fact, the gay sons had lived with their fathers for an average of only six years, whereas the heterosexual sons had lived in the gay father household for almost eleven years. It seems clear that the environment in gay father households is not a factor in the sons' sexual orientation and that the minority (5 to 10 percent) of the gay sons of gay fathers parallels the percentage of gay men in the total population.

GAY PARENTING OVER TIME

Focusing on lesbian mothers, Tasker and Golombok (1997) conducted a longitudinal study that provides valuable insight into the impact of gay parenting on child development. These researchers interviewed mothers and children drawn from two samples: twenty-seven lesbian mothers with thirty-nine children combined and the same number of heterosexual mothers who also had a total of thirty-nine children. Fifteen years later, the researchers were able to get in touch with fifty-one of the original fifty-four mothers and to interview forty-six of their children (with an age range of seventeen to thirty-five years at follow-up). Their findings support the statement that gay parenting does not have an inherent negative impact on child development. In terms of gender identity, gender role, sexual orientation, emotional development, and sexual development, the children raised by lesbian mothers did not differ from those raised by heterosexual mothers. They were no more likely to seek mental health services. They were no more likely to be depressed or anxious. Those with mental health issues had mothers who also had mental health issues. The children of lesbian mothers reported a closer relationship with their mothers' partners than did the children of heterosexual mothers. Although both groups of offspring recall being teased as children, there were no reports of significant teasing about their sexual orientation in either group. This pioneer study provides strong evidence about the generally positive impact of gay parents on their children.

Still, the prevalence of the myths and negative attitudes may negatively affect the relationships that gay fathers can create with their children. Society's uneasiness about gay fathers may be the biggest challenge that gay fathers must overcome. As we continue to examine the experiences and issues that children and gay fathers face, we will take a brief look at the research findings relative to homosexual incest and the fear of "catching" homosexuality.

The concerns that gay fathers will either molest their children or pass along their homosexuality to them reflect an underlying negative attitude about homosexuality: that homosexuals are somehow more sexually undependable with their children than heterosexuals and that homosexuality would be a "bad" thing to catch. Many gay fathers point to the heterosexuality of their own families of origin as a refutation of this concern. One gay father said, "Claiming my sons would catch homosexuality from me is an outrage. If that's the way people become gay, I would be straight. Using this as an excuse to keep my kids from me is just another example of homophobia!" The scant research on these topics indicates that gay fathers do not attempt to influence their children to become homosexuals and that the sexual orientation of the father has little bearing on the child's sexuality (Weeks, Derdeyn, & Langman, 1975).

INFLUENCES ON CHILDREN

In reviewing the impact of gay fathering on children, it is important to acknowledge that most children who live with gay fathers are also the products of divorce and may present psychological distress that typically accompanies families experiencing marital dissolution. All too often the emotional distress of children with a gay parent is attributed solely to the parent's sexual orientation. This is a mistake, given the evidence that children's emotional state results from a complex mixture of family dynamics, divorce adjustment, and incorporation of the parent's sexual coming out (Laird & Green, 1996; Robinson & Chase, 2000).

There are, of course, many issues that are unique to living in a family with a gay father. The societal concerns about the developmental impact on the child of the knowledge that his or her father is homosexual are legitimate and are shared by the gay and lesbian community. The father will have reasonable questions about the need for coming out to his children, and he will need to learn ways to assist his children to minimize the difficulties created by society's negative attitudes about homosexuality. Ben's story at the beginning of the chapter touches on these three issues. There is a possible element of defensiveness in his story that indicates that his overt statements accepting and even prizing his father's sexual orientation may mask a deeper anxiety over how he will cope with this issue as he participates in normal adolescent activities related to his own unfolding sexual relationships with females. Fiona, nineteen, in contrast, seems very clear about her attitude: "Everything about having a gay father is an advantage. I've met lovely people. I wonder how many people with straight parents have as much love as I do and are as happy as I am with my Dad. . . . I can accept people for what they are. . . . Having a gay dad has made me realize that love can manifest itself in so many different ways" (quoted in Saffron, 1996, p. 70).

COMING OUT TO CHILDREN

Coming out to their children is typically an emotion-laden event for gay fathers. Disclosing one's homosexuality to children generates anxiety about possible rejection, fear of damaging the child's self-esteem, and often an awareness that the relationship is about to undergo a fundamental change and that a kind of father relationship will have been lost forever. One father told us,

I knew that my children had not asked to have a father who is gay, and I just could not bring myself to tell them until they became adults. I hoped that by then they would be successfully launched into life and that my lifestyle would have little impact on them. After I first told them they were really angry with me. Finally two of them have come around and seem to want to be a part of my life. The other two are still somewhat wary and reserved. If I could be twenty again, I would probably still marry and have children, for my life with my wife and kids has been deeply meaningful to me. I would not trade the twenty-eight years I spent with them for anything. But now they have their own lives, and I can finally live more of my own life too.

The daughter of another gay father said, "I did not want my father to talk to me about being gay. I knew he was, and I felt violated by that conversation. It would have been easier for me if we had never talked about it. He keeps insisting that I tell him how I feel about it. I just don't want to discuss it at all. I resent it when he brings it up, and sometimes I don't want to be around him."

Another gay father told what had happened in the ten years since he came out to his children:

I have never regretted telling them. It was a hard time for all of us, and I know they wish I were still with their mother. Things had gotten pretty quiet until my oldest daughter came out as a lesbian. That sort of got everything stirred up once more, and everyone was mad at me again.

A couple of years after that, my youngest son and his fiancée asked my daughter and her partner to be in their wedding, so I thought we had finally moved on. But this last year my oldest son wrote me a letter urging me to give my homosexuality to Jesus. I was devastated! And I still don't know how to talk with him. The letters we exchanged got so heated that I decided I would not visit him and his family for a while. I don't think we will ever get over the hurt. I know he loves me and that he wants me to be a grandfather to his children, but I do not think we will ever be close again. I know it is his issue, not mine, and the hardest thing has been to just let it go, to let him go. I hope one day he will understand more fully.

Last week I was driving by a big church here that supports conversion therapy, and I found myself resisting getting out and throwing rocks through every window. I know that would not do any good. But those people who strut around claiming they are Christians and support conversion therapy are hurting lots of families.

I am glad that my relationship with the other two kids is so strong. My lesbian daughter and her partner are so close to me. I love to watch people's faces when I tell them I have one daughter, two sons, and three daughters-in-law. They get this confused look, and I either explain or shrug my shoulders and say, "Go figure" and let them work it out!

No one knows how gay fathers actually do come out to their children. Although they may have come out to themselves and to other members of the gay community and may be involved in clandestine affairs with men, many cite legal and emotional reasons for staying in the closet (Bozett, 1980, 1981a; Humphreys, 1970; Spada, 1979). Others feel that their family roles cannot be reconciled with their sexual orientation, and they never disclose (Bozett, 1981a; Jones, 1978, Ross, 1971). These men lead deeply conflicted lives and probably project their internalized homophobia onto their children as they state, "I am staying married just for my children." Their parenting is characterized by psychological distance, they tend to be more indulgent as a means of resolving some of the guilt they feel over their lack of honesty, and they may become workaholics (Miller, 1979a).

Those fathers who do disclose their sexual orientation do so for a variety of reasons. One man told us, "I like myself as a gay man. It is only natural to want to share that part of who I am with my kids. They will learn something quite valuable from knowing this part of me." This father's comment is consistent with findings that indicate gay fathers value both their role as father (Bozett, 1980) and their sexual identity. As they come to value themselves as homosexuals, it is natural that they would want to share this aspect of themselves with their children. Once a gay man begins to overcome his own internalized fear and shame about being homosexual, he becomes more integrated, and he often reveals his sexual orientation to others. Coming out is one part of developing a positive gay identity, and experts in the field agree that coming out to one's children is seen as an essential part of having integrity as a parent (Barbone & Rice, 1994; Ben-Ari, 1995; Chekola, 1994; Kaufman & Raphael, 1996).

As gay fathers face coming out, their first concern is the well-being and healthy adjustment of their children. Their second worry is that their children, with whom they share perhaps their most significant intimate relationship, will reject them. Although disclosure sometimes initially disturbs the father-child bond, study after study indicates that, in fact, children and fathers become closer after self-disclosure of the father's sexual orientation (Beeler & DiProva, 1999; Bozett, 1980; Miller, 1979a). Several years after learning his father is homosexual, Jim said, "I never knew much about gay men. From my Dad I've learned that gay people are just like all people. I like some of them and don't like others. My likes and dislikes have little to do with their gayness and more to do with who they are. I can see that Dad is happier, and that's what is most important. He has introduced me to people and activities I would have never known about otherwise, and I've learned not to be so judgmental about people who are different."

A father's decision to come out is influenced by several factors. Bigner and Bozett (1990) report that the men they studied weighed several factors as they decided to come out. The major reasons for disclosure the men cited were that they wanted their children to know them as they are; they were aware that the more frequent their contact with their children, the greater the likelihood that the children would discover on their own; and that they had a male partner. Children may also benefit from knowing their father's orientation, as they are then better able to understand what went wrong in the marriage and often no longer feel responsible for the divorce (Miller, 1979a).

Coming Out to Children: Guidelines for Fathers

Bigner and Bozett (1990) drew from the work of Miller (1979a) and Schulenburg (1985) to establish some principles for disclosure of homosexuality to children. These very practical suggestions will be helpful to gay fathers, their children, and mental health professionals.

1. *Come to terms with your own gayness before disclosing to children.* This is critical. If you feel negatively about your homosexuality or are ashamed of it, your children are much more likely to react negatively. You must create a setting of acceptance by first

accepting yourself. If you tell your children when you are ready and comfortable, it is likely to be a positive experience for everyone.

2. *Children are never too young to be told.* They will absorb only as much as they are capable of understanding. Use words appropriate to the age of the child. You can add details as the children grow older.

3. *Discuss it with children before they know or suspect.* If your children discover your sexual orientation from someone other than you, they are likely to be upset that you did not trust them sufficiently to share the information with them. It is exceedingly difficult for children to initiate the subject, and they will not bring it up even though they want to.

4. *Disclosure should be planned.* Children should not find out about your homosexuality by default or discover it accidentally or during an argument between you and their mother.

5. *Disclose in a quiet setting where interruptions are unlikely to occur.*

6. *Inform, don't confess.* The disclosure should not be heavy or maudlin but positive and sincere. Informing in a simple, natural, and matter-of-fact manner when you are ready is more likely to foster acceptance by the child. If possible, discuss or rehearse what you will say to the children with someone who has already experienced a similar disclosure.

7. *Inform the children that relationships with them will not change as a result of disclosure.* Disclosure will, however, allow you to be more honest. Children may need reassurance that you are the same person you were before. Younger children may need reassurance that you will still be their father.

8. *Be prepared for questions.* The following are some questions and possible answers:

- *Why are you telling me this?* Because my personal life is important, and I want to share it with you. I am not ashamed of being homosexual, and you shouldn't be ashamed of me either.

- *What does being gay mean?* It means being attracted to other men so that you might fall in love with a man and express your love physically and sexually.

- *What makes a person gay?* No one knows, although there are a lot of theories. (This question may be a child's way of asking if he or she will also be gay.)

- *Will I be gay, too?* You won't be gay just because I'm gay. It's not contagious, and it doesn't appear to be hereditary. You will be whatever you are going to be.

- *Don't you like women?* I do like women, but I'm not physically (or sexually) and romantically attracted to them as I am to men. (The child might be asking, "Don't you like Mom?" or "Do you hate Mom?" If this question is asked by a daughter, it may also mean "Don't you like me?" or "Do you hate me?")

- *What should I tell my friends about it?* A lot of people just don't understand, so it might be best to keep it in the family. You can discuss it with me any time you want. If you want to tell a close friend, go ahead and try it out. But the friend might not be accepting, and he or she might tell others. You should be prepared for these possibilities. If you do tell somebody, let me know how it turns out.

Gay fathers may come out indirectly (showing affection to men in front of their children or taking their children to gay restaurants and meetings) or directly (verbally or by correspondence) (Maddox, 1982). Sometimes disclosure takes place over time as the father develops a more positive gay identity (Bozett, 1984a) and as the family begins to adjust to the divorce (Bozett, 1981a; Collins & Zimmerman, 1983; Gochros, 1985). Other factors affecting disclosure are the degree of intimacy between the father and his children and the obtrusiveness of his gayness (Bozett, 1988). Children who are told at an earlier age are reported to have fewer difficulties managing the knowledge of their father's homosexuality (Bozett, 1989).

Randy, a gay father, has not yet told his eight-year-old daughter that he is gay even though his ex-wife knows about it, and he lives with his lover, Ian. Randy told us,

> I had worried about being attracted to men, but girls chased me throughout high school and college. Sex with them was OK, so I didn't take my sexual feelings about men seriously. I got married when I was twenty, and Bethany was born two years later.
>
> On a business trip, I found myself having sex with a man, and I knew for sure that I was gay. I didn't tell Mary (my wife) for a while. Instead, I went to my minister and talked to him about it. He had me read the Bible and pray for the feelings to go away. I tried so hard, but could not stay away from men. Mary and I drifted further apart, and I was not surprised when she told me she had fallen in love with someone else and wanted a divorce. That seemed like the perfect solution for both of us.
>
> Later, I found out that after I talked with him (the minister) he called Mary in and told her about me, but we've never talked about it. I have Bethany with me one weekend a month, and I see her each week even though they live seventy miles from here. I am grateful Mary has not stood in the way of my being with my daughter.
>
> I can't imagine how I will ever tell Bethany about me. Recently my lover has been talking about trying to become heterosexual, and our relationship is changing. He is patient when Bethany is here, but he doesn't really like having her around. I worry about what is ahead for all of us.

As Bethany grows older, her awareness of her father's sexual orientation is certain to grow. How the two of them will negotiate his disclosure is uncertain. What is particularly unfortunate in Randy's case is that when he turned to a professional for help, his trust was betrayed. It is doubtful that he will be willing to seek assistance when the day for coming out arrives.

PARENTING STYLES

Findings from the research suggest that both gay and heterosexual men experience parenthood for similar reasons (Bigner & Jacobsen, 1989b). But gay fathers try harder to create stable home lives and positive relationships with their children than one would expect from traditional heterosexual parents (Bozett, 1989). Children living in families with a homosexual parent have the same issues as children living in more conventional families. Harris and Turner (1986) interviewed twenty-three gay and lesbian parents and sixteen heterosexual single parents and found few differences in their parenting. Both homosexual and heterosexual subjects reported only a minimal number of serious problems and characterized their relationships with their children as mostly positive. The only noticeable difference was an increased concern among heterosexual parents about their children's exposure to opposite-sex role models. These researchers conclude that being homosexual is compatible with effective parenting and is not usually a major issue in parental relationships with children.

Another study comparing gay and heterosexual fathers found that gay men were more nurturing, were less traditional in paternal attitudes, and described themselves as functioning more positively as fathers than did heterosexual fathers (Scallen, 1981). Although heterosexual fathers in this study placed more emphasis on their role as economic provider, no differences between the two groups were reported in parental problem solving, recreation, or encouragement of autonomy.

In another study of gay fathers, Bigner and Jacobsen (1989a) found no differences in parental involvement and amount of intimacy in the sixty-six fathers they sampled (thirty-three homosexual, thirty-three heterosexual). Gay fathers in this study differed significantly in that they used more reasoning, were more responsive to their children's behaviors, and were stricter in setting limits for their children. The investigators attributed their findings to possible beliefs among gay fathers that they must be better parents to overcome potential hardships resulting from the father's sexuality. They must run a tight ship in the execution of their control over their kids because they feel they are being scrutinized more closely than other fathers because of their sexual orientation. These conclusions are similar to other reports of the experience of noncustodial single fathers (Robinson & Barret, 1986).

Findings of no difference between homosexual and heterosexual fathers do not mean that the experience of having a gay father is risk-free. Miller (1979a) found that six daughters of the gay fathers in his study had significant life problems (pregnancy, prostitution, and school and emotional difficulties). Other reports indicate that children with gay fathers are exposed to ridicule and harassment (Bozett, 1980; Epstein, 1979) or may become alienated from their age mates, become confused about their sexual identity, and express discomfort with their fathers' sexual orientation (Lewis, 1980). Remember that these responses may not be solely related to the sexuality of the father; these children have lost whatever stability their family life offered them. Their problems are surely a result of adjusting to a mixture of very complex issues at crucial developmental phases.

DEALING WITH THE OUTSIDE WORLD

Gay fathers and their children live in a larger world, one that is definitely not hospitable to gay men and lesbians and certainly not generally supportive of gay parenting. One facet of coming out as a gay father is planning ways to successfully interact with the world of schools, PTAs, churches, scouts, athletic and cultural events, and social networks. Adapting to the realities of a homophobic world, gay fathers often see no choice other than to continue living relatively closeted lives (Miller, 1979a; Bozett, 1988). The gay father's desire to help his children develop a positive attitude about homosexuality conflicts with the caution against his children letting teachers and friends know about his homosexuality. Some fathers deal with this by placing their children in schools outside the neighborhood (Strommen, 1989). Others, fearing the exposure of a possible custody battle based on their homosexuality, live tightly controlled lives or simply never develop their gay identity. The overall thrust, however, is one to protect their children from the adverse effects that often follow public disclosure. At the same time, many of these fathers attempt to help their children develop a positive gay sensitivity rather than allow them to take on society's negative homosexual labeling (Morin & Schultz, 1978; Riddle, 1978).

Bozett (1988) identified several strategies that children employ as they encounter their own and the public's discomfort with gay fathers. Bozett found that children of gay fathers use boundary control (control of the father in relation to the self, control of the self in relation to the father, and control of others in relation to the father), nondisclosure, and disclosure strategies as they interact with their gay fathers and the outside world. Among the major reasons subjects gave for not disclosing their father's gayness was the fear that their identity would become contaminated by their peers thinking that if their father is gay, they must be gay, too. Interviews with children of gay parents indicate that children who do disclose often are taunted by being called "queer" and "fag." This concern is particularly evident when the children are in their adolescent years (Riddle & Arguelles, 1981). The child's choice of social control strategy is influenced by the degree of intimacy between parent and child, whether or not the child resides with the father, and the maturity of the child.

Obviously, children with gay fathers must carefully consider the consequences as they decide who and how to inform others of their father's sexual orientation. Keeping this important aspect of their lives secret means they may live highly compartmentalized lives, and when they seek mental services, they may present feelings of isolation and alienation. Nondisclosure can also lead to an effort to control the gay father's behavior. Asking the father to remove all evidence of his sexual orientation from the home and setting boundaries that separate the child's and the father's social groups may be exceedingly difficult. Such expectations undermine the new gay identity that gay fathers are attempting to construct and reflect a sense of shame that the father's life is wrong and should be hidden. Fathers who remove all evidence of their sexual orientation must basically erase who they truly are.

CONCLUSIONS

In summary, the limited research findings indicate that children of homosexual fathers do not differ significantly from children reared in more traditional families. They appear to accept their fathers as gay and find ways to integrate this uniqueness into their lives. We can draw the following conclusions about children of homosexual fathers:

- They are like all kids. Some will excel, some will have problems, some will be average.

- They live in a significantly different home environment and must develop strategies to deal with it.

- They may need help sorting out their own feelings about homosexuality.

- They may be isolated and angry.

- They are not likely to become homosexual.

- They are in little danger of sexual abuse.

- Many of them adjust to this family system and use it to learn about an aspect of humanity they might otherwise ignore.

- There is an opportunity for them to become not only tolerant but also supportive of a positive gay identity.

- Their relationships with their fathers are reported as being more honest and open.

After extensive interviews with sons and daughters of gay men and lesbians, Saffron (1996, p. 183) reported the following:

- Children with gay or lesbian parents do not need for their parents to be heterosexual, do not need to have parents of both sexes, and do need for their parents to be happy.

- Children are happier with parents who have an equal relationship.

- Children learn positive moral values from their lesbian and gay parents.

TIPS FOR PRACTITIONERS

Mental health professionals who interact with children of gay fathers need to be prepared much in the same way fathers prepare themselves for disclosure. (Refer to the guidelines on page 91.) It is important for you to model gay-positive attitudes that reflect an alternative lifestyle with unique richness and diversity. By expressing such gay-positiveness while at the same time realistically expressing the difficulties inherent in any alternative lifestyle, you will enable the child to explore all aspects of his or her situation. The following guidelines represent a synthesis of this chapter.

Help Children Separate Sexual Orientation Issues from Divorce Issues

The child's emotional crisis is likely to be based in a complex reaction to a major life change. His or her feelings related to the parental separation or divorce as well as to the father's sexuality are likely to be intertwined. Carefully help the child separate these issues by exploring the extent to which each situation is distressing.

Further, the reactions of parents and the extended families can serve as secure anchors or sources of distress for children. For example, children who are caught in the cross fire of one family system that wants to totally exclude their father and another that either tolerates or welcomes him may report conflicted loyalties. Their distress may be more related to this disparity than to their father's sexuality. During any major change, children will benefit from the maintenance of routines that allow them to experience predictability and control. Access to both parents during this change will be stabilizing.

Inform Children About the Grieving Process

Children, like adults, may need help sorting out their feelings about homosexuality (based on their own experiences) and the negative stereotypes so prevalent throughout the world. You can help by providing age-appropriate information about homosexuality and gay fathers. Adjustment to any life change is a process. It is important to validate and legitimize whatever feelings children may present as their reaction to what has happened. At the same time, it could help to let them know that this adjustment is part of an ongoing process and that they may develop quite different feelings over time. You need to explore expressions of anger and betrayal at the father for his deception. Be ready to work on issues of grief and loss of the nuclear family as well as of the father's heterosexuality.

Help Resolve Conflicts Between Inner Feelings and Society's Homonegativity

Children of gay fathers will need assistance in resolving the disparity between filial love and society's negative message about homosexuals. Many of these children are in a bind as they express feelings of love for their fathers and at the same time recognize that the world at large sometimes holds contempt for these men. Helping children realize that being homosexual is more than simply having sex with men is the first step in introducing them to the diversity inherent in this subculture. Presenting the gay family as one part of the spectrum of the alternative lifestyles movement of the early 2000s will put the child's experience in perspective. For example, the child will find it reassuring to identify the different types of families he or she has been exposed to.

Allay Children's Fears of Homophobia and Heterosexism

Children may need to be reassured that their father's sexual orientation does not automatically mean that they will be homosexual also. Children may need help formulating responses to inquisitive outsiders as well as support in keeping their fathers' homosexuality a secret. Children also may need help in exploring ways to communicate their feelings in a direct manner. They may need to learn how to stand up for themselves in the new family system or learn how to sensitize their fathers to their discomfort at observing kissing or other physical expressions of affection between men.

Facilitate the Coming-Out Process

Before becoming involved in work with children, you may find yourself assisting a gay father in planning his coming out to his children. Having him examine how to give this information as well as express what he needs from his children are two important parts of this process. Encourage him to rehearse with you what he will say.

Use Role Models

Some children live with gay parents who chose parenting in full awareness of their homosexuality. These children grow up in households where the father's homosexuality has been a daily part of their lives. Openly gay men who become parents through surrogate mothers, adoption, or other legal means typically are focused on the well-being of their children but also are less afraid of losing custody if their sexual orientation becomes known. These families often can serve as role models for other gay families.

Provide Support Groups for Children

Many of these children live in families that have become isolated from the mainstream. Their reactions to being different often cause them to avoid including their peers in their home environments. Referring them to a support group for children in gay families can reduce some of their isolation. If such groups are not available, giving them information about the existence of these groups in other cities can help "normalize" their experience. Some gay fathers also become isolated because they fear disclosure would mean a loss of custody. These families may devote significant energy to "keeping the secret." That can include sending children to schools out of the neighborhood or having no social life that incorporates their home lives. Use the resources in the Appendix to help children contact organizations or read literature that will give them more perspective on their situations.

Focus on Similarities Rather Than Differences

Recognizing that gay families are very similar to more traditional families is important. Gay families show evidence of love and concern just like other families; they adjust to divorce just like other families; and their postdivorce reorganization creates similar strains and opportunities. The gay family can be a source of growth for all who encounter it and can serve as a most appropriate learning forum for developing respect for all types of people.

5

Gay Male Relationships, Spiritual Issues, and Gay Grandfathers

Mike was married for eleven years. During this time he avowed he was not interested in being a father. Following his divorce he began a committed relationship with Robin, a man who had a young daughter. (Robin's story is presented in Chapter Two.) Several years later Michael writes about being a stepfather, an experience he had never imagined he would love.

During my eleven-year marriage to a female, I vowed never to have children. I remember bristling at the often-heard question, "When are you two going to start a family?" I repeatedly told people that I did not need children to validate me and that some families are made up of two people. Shortly after my thirty-fourth birthday I began struggling with my sexual orientation, something I had suppressed, or tried to suppress, for too long. I watched my wife, who was two years older, realize that her childbearing years were drawing to a close. I felt bad about so many things, especially of depriving a woman who would be a great mother of the opportunity to have children. I also began to realize that she was giving up that experience because she loved me and did not want to push me away. Without telling her, I started going to counseling, and it did not take too long for me to know that pretending I was straight was not fair to her. Gayle and I went on vacation, and I told her what was going on with me. I had developed horrible visions of that moment; and, as a matter of fact, it was pretty horrible for both of us. But over the next month as we talked about it more, I learned so much about the true love and respect we had for each other. You know, she never "outed" me to anybody. It was not long after that when we separated and then divorced.

I dated for approximately a year before I met Robin at a charity event. Actually I just saw him across the room, and, as corny as it may seem, I knew in a moment that he was the one for me. I got into great contortions trying to figure out how to meet him, but fate took care of me, and I happened to run into him at church the next Sunday. In getting to know him, I asked what he had done over the weekend. He smiled and said he had spent the weekend with his one-year-old daughter. In spite of the years of disavowing children, I remember a warm glow inside knowing that this man, to whom I felt such a strong attraction, had a child.

We went out for three weeks before it was obvious that we had decided to live together. Somehow it just felt right for both of us, and we could hardly spend time apart. And, of course, the day came when I met Tyler. I don't know who was more afraid when I first picked her up. I didn't really know how to act around her, but I guess I pulled it off OK. The initial problem was that Robin and his wife had separated but no papers had been signed, and no firm agreements had been reached about child custody. We both knew that my presence in his life could be a threat to his access to Tyler. Soon I found myself slinking into restaurants with Robin, afraid that if his wife knew he was seeing a man, all hopes of joint custody were gone. I will never forget an incident when the three of us were at church. Tyler was asleep in his lap, and his wife's lawyer sat down beside us. Fortunately he did not know Robin, but I saw the fear in Robin's eyes as we went up for communion. I prayed so hard that something good would come out of that threat.

And you know what? Once again I learned that our fears are so much greater than the reality of our experience. Nothing came from that experience at church. As we relaxed more and more into our relationship, I began the process of getting to know Tyler. I had always been uncertain about what to say to children, but as we spent more and more time together I began to relax. Before long I was reading to her just like she was my natural daughter. For me, not only had I made the transition from a straight to a gay relationship, but suddenly I found myself involved with a child on a regular basis. At times I feel stunned at the major changes in my life, but I would not give up the experience of parenting Tyler. She has taught me a lot, and I would not trade this time with her for anything.

Of course, there have been several "tests" of our relationship. Robin and I have worked hard to establish an effective relationship with Tyler's mom. We consult with professionals to understand more fully the way parenting and our relationship interact. There have been lots of frustrations for all of us. When we bought a new house, I jumped into planning the garden and was having a great time until Robin asked where the play area was going to be. I responded quickly, "Behind the garage. We don't want to spoil the garden with a swing set!" We had to see our counselor to work that one out, and now our garden has a visible but tasteful play area where we can watch Tyler play.

Finding a counselor who knows anything about gay parenting has been a struggle. Maybe we are like most stepfamilies, but I don't think too many mental health professionals have a clue about the dynamics of a same-sex relationship. We've read some books on child development, and I began to understand that much of what was going on was the natural process of Tyler's development. I began to relax when she would cling to Robin or would shout at me, "I want Daddy to do it!" Actually those incidents have very little to do with me and just are expressions of her growing personality.

Being her stepfather has also brought up some of my unresolved childhood issues. Once when I was picking her up at kindergarten I found myself surrounded by four-year-olds. The anxiety that rose up in me had nothing to do with her but came from memories of my own interactions with others when I was her age. I began to understand that one of the reasons I had avoided children came from my own unresolved childhood issues.

There are still times when parenting collides with our relationship, but Robin and I work hard in our commitment to have a strong family life. Sometimes I find myself competing with a five-year-old for his attention and watching as Robin gets torn in two. Having never had to share Gayle with a child, sometimes I get impatient when Robin chooses to respond to Tyler's needs first. I hear lots of gay fathers saying, "My children come first." I often wonder how their partners find their place when the gay parent has that attitude. Robin's statement has always been, "My family comes first," and I know without a doubt that I am a part of this family. Robin never has stopped me from disciplining her, and we have learned to make decisions jointly so that she will grow up seeing us support each other as her parents.

My parents treat Tyler as one of their grandchildren. At first I was nervous when we began having my family and Robin's together at our home. But now they interact just like any other in-laws, and all the nieces and nephews love to come to our house for special occasions. We truly are a family, and I feel so lucky when I experience all of the love we share. I never thought I would be looking for a church that has a strong program for children. But that has been easy, and I know that our joint spiritual life will further strengthen our family life.

As an attorney who specializes in domestic law, I have had many gay and lesbian parents seek my assistance in their divorces. Unfortunately, in North Carolina, the laws governing custody of children where one of the parents is in a live-in same-sex relationship are not reassuring. So far, we have maintained open lines of communication with Tyler's mother and have worked well together. I can only hope the North Carolina court's attitude toward same-sex parenting will change as Tyler becomes an adolescent.

Life is certainly different with Tyler, but it is a difference I choose. I am in love with a wonderful man, and I try very hard to be a stepparent to a beautiful little girl. The irony of it all is that my ex-wife has chosen not to have children. She would be startled to see Tyler and me sitting on the front steps reading stories, painting fingernails, and playing with Barbies. I hope she would sigh with relief in realizing that the Barbies are not mine.

Mike
Charlotte, North Carolina

STEPPARENTING AND GAY MALE RELATIONSHIPS

Nongay persons who think about same-sex relationships at all probably either are caught in the stereotype that suggests that all gay men are driven by uncontrollable sexual energy or assume that a same-sex relationship could not look like an opposite-sex one. Both of these assumptions would be incorrect. Gay men form relationships that are both similar to and different from those of their nongay peers. And their relationships are no more or less sex centered than any others. Still, their relationships are unique, and it is that uniqueness that is of interest to us.

In a list of ten common issues presented by gay couples in therapy, McVinney (1998, p. 210) includes the following:

- Conflicts associated with differences in stages of being out around their gay identity

- Conflicts associated with differences in extended family involvement

- Conflicts associated with perceived inequalities of power and difficulty in negotiating

- Conflicts associated with finances and financial disparity

Coming out is a lifelong process for gay men, and when the two partners are at different stages, tension can develop. For example, if Robin were not out to his family and Mike were, we could expect numerous conflicts. How to spend holidays and how to help Tyler not talk to one set of grandparents about her time with Robin (or Mike would simply not be present when she was around) would create tension. If Mike were out at work and Robin were not, conflicts could arise over Robin's going alone to business-related social events. If Robin were not out to his ex-wife, once again Tyler might be in the position of keeping a secret, or Mike would have to have somewhere to go on the weekends when Tyler was with Robin.

Gay relationships evolved during a time when many gay people were in the closet. Not having access to legal marriage, these relationships have taken on very personal and distinct characteristics. Issues that have to be resolved include how money will be handled, whether or not property will be owned jointly, and in the case of a gay father, inheritance distributions. Will the spouse inherit a trust that will be passed on to the children, or will the spouse be left out of a will so that everything will go to the children? How will the gay couple negotiate time spent with the children? If the couple's finances have been merged, does the gay father have the right to spend on his children without consulting with his partner? Finally, extended family on one side might be very supportive and the other might be distant. If this is the case, will the couple be able to negotiate holiday and vacation time with extended family?

The responsibilities of parenting may mean that the gay father has to have more involvement with his extended family or that financial commitments to children may take priority over the couple's spending, thereby giving the father more power in the relationship. Further, if the gay father is more closeted in an effort to protect his children, the more "out" partner may resent being back in the closet. One stepfather said,

> I don't know how this happened to me. The other men I have dated have not demanded so much compromise. I feel like I am stuck in a straight lifestyle and that my contacts with gay friends have been severely limited because he is so uptight about being seen with me in

public. And so much of his money goes to his son. We can't replace
our worn-out car because he has to pay for child care. I did not know
it was going to be so difficult. Many times I feel pushed out by
his son. I love both of them, but I was not prepared for this kind of
sacrifice.

Just as Mike in the chapter-opening story had to deal with feelings of jealousy and sometimes felt he had to compete with Tyler to
get Robin's attention, this father struggles with trying to find his
place in the relationship.

Very early in the relationship, gay fathers and their partners must
resolve such issues as how time will be spent, suburban versus urban
living, discipline, relationships with ex-wives, introducing step-
grandparents and integrating the extended families, and managing
school and other child-care activities. As the relationship develops,
the couple must give particular attention to the ways cohabiting
will affect the new family and the role of children in commitment
ceremonies. Those couples who have become parents through adoption face critical decisions about who will be the legal parent. Most
states will not allow coadoption of children, and the partner who is
named as the primary parent will have to move very carefully to
keep the balance of power even.

SUPPORT SYSTEMS

Other challenges that face gay families include the negative impact
of living in a stigmatized community, the lack of legal support for gay
relationships, the failure of schools and other organizations to train
their employees in ways to assist gay and lesbian parents, the threat
of loss of paternal rights because of being in an openly gay relationship, and issues of secrecy necessitated when an ex-spouse may use
the father's sexual orientation to gain sole custody. Our social system
has not yet developed informed strategies for integrating gay fathers

and their partners into their institutional practices. One professional related his experience in a custody hearing: "I was asked to be an expert witness on behalf of the gay father who was seeking joint custody of his four sons. His ex-wife's attorney would object to almost every question I was asked. Finally the judge told me to go on and answer. She had looked for information on gay parenting's effects on children and could not find anything. She asked me to review the literature for her. Somehow our legal system has got to get informed about the realities of gay parenting."

Few educational programs for attorneys, teachers, physicians, or school principals and counselors include discussions of effective ways to help gay or lesbian stepfamilies, and when these families come for counseling, often the quality of the interaction is poor. A school counselor reported the following dilemma. An eighth-grade boy, Jerome, was being teased by his peers because they learned his father is gay. The counselor had previously met with the father, who told her about his sexual orientation and asked that she notify him if there was any trouble. Obviously distressed, Jerome came to see the counselor but would only allude to a "secret" that had gotten out. Over and over he said, "I will never trust anyone again." The counselor did not tell Jerome that his father had come to see her and that she knew the father was gay. She met with Jerome for several weeks, afraid to tell him that she knew the secret. In supervision she began to understand that her negative beliefs about gay parents were stopping her from giving Jerome the kind of support he needed. Once the counselor was able to let him know that she knew the "secret," Jerome began to find the support and understanding he needed in order to move on.

Although the experiences of the members of gay families mimic those of their straight brothers and sisters, a fundamentally unique underlying challenge is that they live in communities that do not approve of the father's relationship (Baptiste, 1988; Beeler & DiProva, 1999). Further, their parenting takes place in an atmosphere of suspicion generated by others' discomfort around two men living together with children. LaSala (1998) interviewed forty men who constituted twenty gay couples about their family's reaction to the relationship. His findings were that one or both members of the couple experienced antagonism from their parents or parents-in-law. All of the myths about homosexuality (see Chapter Two) come into play as these families interact with their neighbors. This oppression and negative bias can become a daily experience for gay stepfamilies, one that places much stress on the nonbiological father.

One area of particular concern for gay couples who adopt is what will happen to the children if the relationship ends. Many social workers who are trying to place children in gay families suggest that the adopting father identify himself as single. Laws vary from state to state, and so far Vermont and Massachusetts are the only states that allow second-parent adoption by gay couples. Other states, such as California, Washington, Illinois, and Indiana, have cases in the pipeline, and in some counties second-parent adoption may be allowed. These laws can change rapidly, and the only way to know for sure in a specific instance is to consult an attorney. This means that even though an adopted child may live with a couple for five or ten years, only the adoptive father can have custody if the relationship fails. And, just as in heterosexual relationships, sometimes the "divorce" involves much dispute over access to the children.

As time passes and more gay men adopt children, and the courts become more familiar with the absence of negative impact from gay parenting, this situation will improve. Stepparenting, which is quickly becoming the dominant family structure in the United States, is a difficult challenge for all couples, straight and gay (Howell, Weers, & Kleist, 1998). Unless gay couples have very strong communication and a solid understanding of the demands of parenting, they may flounder as they try to parent together.

SPIRITUAL ISSUES

Gay men face unique spiritual challenges. If they participate in religious life, they may seek out churches, synagogues, or other religious organizations that are open to them, or they may go back into the closet when they attend services. Many gay men reject organized religion as a whole because of the judgmental and rejecting rhetoric they have been subjected to as they grew up. Still others drift toward New Age religions that are more accepting, and some even investigate paganism or other nontraditional religious groups.

These choices may not be satisfactory for gay fathers who want their children to have a traditional religious experience. Men like Robin (Chapter Two) are determined to participate in religious organizations both for personal reasons and to offer their children religious instruction. A particular problem for gay fathers is that many churches condemn homosexuality, and these men are reluctant to expose their children to institutions that portray their fathers as sinful outcasts. The Metropolitan Community Church (MCC) is a Christian denomination that has grown out of the gay community. Active in most major cities, the MCC has congregations that are predominantly, but not exclusively, gay and lesbian, but only in rare instances do they offer children's programs. Fortunately there are increasing numbers of traditional religious institutions that are becoming aware of an opportunity to welcome sexual minorities into their membership. And although these churches and synagogues rarely extend programming exclusively to sexual minorities, they welcome them to participate in virtually all aspects of religious life. In just about every denomination, one can find a congregation that has taken the step of being identified as a "welcoming congregation."

You need not look too far into the major religious groups in the United States today to become aware of the often intense debate about the role of gay men and lesbians in the church. In most religious organizations, you can find evidence of debate about the nature of homosexuality and the place of gay men and lesbians in worship. As recently as 1998, Pope John Paul II, although clearly still viewing gay men and lesbians as sinners, urged Catholic parents to love their gay sons and lesbian daughters. Although not yet able to see homosexuality as a normal human experience, the Catholic Church and other Christian and Jewish groups are beginning to understand that just being gay or lesbian does not automatically cast one out. Rather, as these institutions include gay men and lesbians, they are learning that both gay and nongay people have more in common than they had thought. As a result there is a steady debate about the limits to such welcoming efforts. What will happen if we allow gay men and lesbians to become pastors? What would happen if those already ordained lived an openly gay life? How many will leave the church because they disapprove of a more modern understanding of homosexuality? Is it safer to offend gay men and lesbians than our heterosexual membership? Questions like these are complex, and religious organizations move slowly.

Just about every major religion in the world expresses uneasiness about homosexuality. Relying on scripture and traditions that have been historically interpreted as condemning of homosexuality, these groups have been silent or have denounced and branded homosexuals as sinners. Naturally we see this latter response most easily in the more fundamental and conservative groups. Jerry Falwell and Pat Robertson issue vindictive pronouncements about the threat of homosexuals to the traditional family. Also identified with the anti-gay movement, many other religious groups share their view, even though they may be less vociferous in their public exhortations. Gay fathers who have grown up in these churches and synagogues often become "alumni" of organized religion. And in their father role they struggle with the dilemma of exposing their children to such negative understandings. One father told us,

I really don't know what to do about Sally. I grew up in the Catholic Church, and I was a total believer. As I began to realize that I am gay, I did not know what to do. I spoke to my priest about it, and he was totally condemning. I left the church feeling very confused and hurt. And over the years I began to see the way the church oppresses lots of people, not just gays. Today I am bitter and mistrustful of any church. Still, I want Sally to know what religion is all about. Recently I have been attending a Quaker meeting. In that organization there is a national group of gay men and lesbians who meet once a year, and I'm planning on going next year. I like sitting in the hour of silence where neither Sally nor I have to listen to preachers ranting and raving about "those condemned homosexuals." I also like that she is being exposed to a religious practice that allows for a lot of personal exploration. Would I consider going back to the Catholic Church? Not on your life!

Others decide never to go back to a religious practice. Al and his wife had divorced after he spoke with his minister about his homosexuality. The minister broke the confidentiality of this disclosure and went to Al's wife and told her about him. Within days, Al had been thrown out of the house and denied access to his six-year-old daughter Tiffany. Ten years later, Al had reestablished a relationship with his daughter, who still attends the same church with the same minister. In considering coming out to Tiffany, Al said,

I don't know what to do. That minister could tell her at any time, and I want her to hear it from me. She seems so staunch in her acceptance of everything the minister says. I've never seen her question any of it. And I worry that she will be totally confused about how to react to me. One time when she was here for a visit, she made a negative comment about gay men. I asked her where she had learned that, and she replied, "At church. Gay people are condemned by God." I'd like to expose her to a different view but am not sure there is a church that is safe. When she comes for a visit, my partner stays with friends, and I hide pictures of us together or other things that she might wonder about. Naturally he does not like being away, but so far he seems to understand.

Five years later Al died of HIV disease. Toward the end, he did have a talk with Tiffany; she told him he was a sinner and refused to attend his funeral.

Manuel, in contrast, came out to his daughter with the support of his priest. After he and Consuela had their conversation, the priest also met with them to talk further about how she might understand this news. Now he and Consuela attend Mass together, and he has even taken her to a special service for gay men and their families. This way she has learned that there are other kids with gay parents and that they are welcome in the church despite the general social uneasiness about homosexuality.

On the whole, if one were to stand back and observe nongay parents and gay fathers, the similarities between them would be obvious. Many attend traditional religious organizations, others seek out more creative expressions of their spirituality, and some belong to New Age groups that are more accepting of diversity (Barret & Barzan, 1996, 1997). Those who are visible in traditional groups may identify themselves as gay, but many remain in the closet, perhaps not understanding the negative influences that such internalized oppression can have on them and their children. Some abandon all spiritual experience because they do not want to face the negative comments and possible rejection they experienced in the past. For others, reconciling their sexual orientation with religion is simply too complex and a painful ordeal (for example, White, 1994).

Those who live in the closet and join traditional religious groups may face unexpected challenges. Dwight described what happened to him when his son, Jimmy, came to live with him:

I had never expected to be a full-time father. Jimmy and his mother lived five hundred miles from me. He would come for visits, and I managed that quite well. I had been very active in a Methodist church and was even the scoutmaster for their troop. When Jimmy's mom called and told me she could not deal with him any longer, I immediately told her to send him to me. He had not known I was gay, and I knew that having a teenager in the house and expecting to keep this a secret was impossible. So, shortly after he got here I came out to him. He took it just fine, asked a few questions, and that was it. But I was in a panic about what to do at church. I did not want him to see my own homophobia. I was not going to tell him not to tell others. So

I had to either find another church or just come out there too. I talked
with my minister, who was supportive of my coming out, but only
after I had resigned from the scouts. I was hurt by that, but I went
along. At the time it seemed best for Jimmy and me. Now I would do
it differently.

Evidence of oppression at the hands of religious organizations
abounds (Goss, 1993; White 1994). A predominantly gay congregation in the Evangelical Lutheran Church was expelled from the
denomination when they appointed an openly lesbian woman as
one of their ministers. A gay father balks at the idea of coming out
to his family: "First they are going to condemn me to hell, then I
will have to leave our church because they will not allow me to worship as long as I am gay. And then they will threaten to take my
daughter from me. Sometimes I feel like I am lying to God, and that
is the worst thing I can do. How can I live as a gay father and teach
my daughter that being gay is OK and still practice my faith?"

Larry and Stephen have been together for seventeen years and
worship with Stephen's teenage sons at a prominent church in their
community. Stephen speaks of an upcoming church service that
will include the marriage of a nongay couple who are also church
members.

I don't know why the church is doing this. We have to sit through all
of the celebrations of heterosexuality: baptisms, confirmations . . . and
now this wedding! Even though the preacher blesses members' pets
each year, he will not even consider saying a prayer over our relationship. I feel like they are constantly reminding my sons and me that
being gay is being second class. I urged them to have a special service that would honor nontraditional families. There are plenty of never-
married straight people who are also left out of these events. But the
answer was, "We're not ready for that. You must be patient." I have
almost had it with being patient, and I'd just walk away, but my sons
like it there. They know I am upset but don't say anything about it.

The local and national media frequently carry reports of religious organizations voting on some aspect of homosexuality. Will we ordain homosexuals? If they are welcome in our congregations, is it reasonable for us to ask them to declare a commitment to celibacy? Do we let them participate in the sacraments even though technically what they are doing has been declared a sin? Do we bless their relationships? And if we welcome them into our congregations, do we make special efforts to assist their children? Do we have to accept them as "normal" parents? How do we reconcile our own feelings about this with the official positions taken by our national leadership? Is there a way to learn more about this group without approving their lifestyles?

In communities across the nation the media will turn to a religious figure to comment when there is a gay issue being covered. These respondents have little formal training about the intricacies of sexual orientation and typically make statements that affirm that being gay is a moral issue that links homosexuality to sin. These church officials often unknowingly sit shoulder to shoulder with closeted homosexual men and women who fear they must protect their bureaucratic positions in the church hierarchy at all costs (White, 1994).

Fortunately not all religious groups take this approach. Some want to take steps toward understanding more fully the lives of gay men and lesbians (Johnson, 1992). It is possible, largely in inner-city religious organizations, for gay and lesbian parents to find safe places for their families. These groups often have very visible gay and lesbian members and rarely seem to attack them as outcasts. Some ministers and rabbis even use gay and lesbian examples in their sermons and prayers. Others may not be quite so bold but make it clear that everyone is welcome and that they are not interested in condemning anyone on the basis of sexual orientation. Likewise there is a growing body of literature on the issue of sexual minorities and religion (Alexander & Preston, 1996; Comstock, 1996; Eger, 1992; Nugent, 1992; Gomes, 1996; Seow, 1996; Whitehead, 1997).

Resolving Spiritual and Religious Conflicts

A fundamental struggle is for gay men and lesbians to find ways to overcome the clash between homoprejudiced religious institutions that assert their authority and personal spiritual experiences that connect them with a Supreme Being who offers love and acceptance. For many gay clients this struggle begins in adolescence. In most religious groups, adolescents are carefully taught ways to integrate their emerging sexuality into their religious lives. Church youth groups often provide closely chaperoned opportunities for boys and girls to socialize. Retreats, camps, and other venues where adolescents mix further the church's teachings about heterosexual relationships. Such nurturing is not available for most gay and lesbian youth. Rather than being encouraged to embrace their sexuality, most gay youth learn to hate and fear their sexuality. Deprived of assistance from families, schools, and churches in learning how to affirm both themselves and their sexual orientation, and feeling pressure to live up to the family expectations to learn a particular religious orthodoxy, many gay youth come to compartmentalize their sexual orientation. Outwardly they participate in their religious organizations, yet inwardly they are involved in a sometimes powerful struggle to reconcile their religious beliefs with their emerging sexual identity. Safe in the compartment, some remain unconscious about their gayness; others hope that through prayer or "being good," God will take away this demon. Others completely reject religious institutions and turn their search inward to a personal spiritual experience, and some resort to an active search for another, more accepting religious organization.

Gay and lesbian clients may struggle with renouncing the authority of the church as well as with finding ways to affirm the lessons of inclusive and spiritual connectedness that come from their authentic spiritual experience. As a counselor, you may find that assisting gay men and lesbians to step away from external religious authority challenges your own acceptance of religious teachings.

Fortunately, gay men and lesbians frequently have experience in claiming the primacy of their own authority. D'Augelli (1992) points out that because they often feel different from other family members, they learn to separate early from the family. As they acknowledge a sexual orientation that may lead to rejection by their families, they have learned to trust their own experiences rather than the dictates of the family. D'Augelli's work suggests that this early emancipation enables gay men and lesbians to become independent as they create their life goals. Others may push themselves to achieve as a way to compensate for what has been labeled a deficit. As a counselor working with gay men and lesbians who are exploring their spiritual beliefs, you can draw an analogy between clients' need to rely on an internal understanding that leads them to live contrary to their families' wishes and the similar task that they can undertake with an authoritarian religious organization. As you and your client explore these topics it is important for both of you to understand the need for creative resolutions to this dynamic. Encouraging gay clients to look beyond the confines of the religious worldview they may have learned as children is equally important. Celebrating the spiritual aspects of everyday life and pointing out that personal authenticity and adherence to truth are significant spiritual values can be a point of emancipation (Barzan, 1995). Assisting with understanding that an ability to love a person of the same sex is indeed a great spiritual blessing may help gay clients affirm their sexual identity.

Most counselors benefit from using a model that distinguishes between spiritual and religious authority. In separating these two experiences, clients are better able to see that their own life events can be a source of authority. A model that will help clients work through the shame, guilt, and condemnation espoused by many religious groups is essential. The model illustrated in Figure 5.1 will help clients actively explore a gay-positive spiritual world with a greater internal sense of authenticity and integrity.

Understanding that metaphysical experience takes many forms and that what we call spirituality and religiosity may be quite different experiences allows the client to add flexibility to previously rigid positions. Like all people, gay men and lesbians have the capacity to affirm their own spiritual experiences as more direct and possibly even more valid spiritual experiences that lead them toward Truth.

It seems appropriate to add the reminder here that religion is one of an almost infinite number of expressions of one's personal and communal spirituality, and Christianity is but one among many world religions. Learning about other religious traditions can be helpful; realizing the meaning that can be found in non-Western traditions, such as Buddhism and Islam, or even dismissing the religious canon entirely, is essential. (The foregoing discussion was adapted from Barret & Barzan, 1996.)

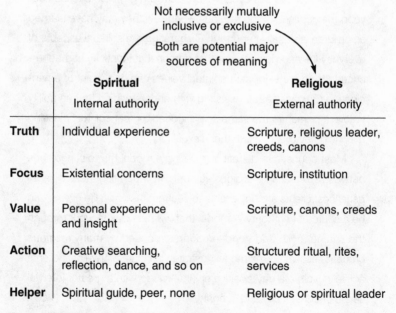

	Spiritual Internal authority	**Religious** External authority
Truth	Individual experience	Scripture, religious leader, creeds, canons
Focus	Existential concerns	Scripture, institution
Value	Personal experience and insight	Scripture, canons, creeds
Action	Creative searching, reflection, dance, and so on	Structured ritual, rites, services
Helper	Spiritual guide, peer, none	Religious or spiritual leader

Figure 5.1. Spiritual and Religious Dichotomy

As early as 1984, Catholic theologian Matthew Fox outlined a four-step process of spiritual development for gay men and lesbians: (1) creation, in which the person truly embraces the gay self; (2) letting go, in which the person acknowledges and releases the pain of rejection; (3) creativity that leads to the rebirth of the soul; and (4) transformation, in which the person extends compassion and a sense of celebration to others. These steps mirror the coming-out process but employ a different language.

Unfortunately, few organizations have accepted Fox's thoughts. Gay fathers who participate in religious communities display needs similar to those of their nongay peers: they seek a sense of something greater than self, a sense of community, answers to universal questions, and moral guidance (Perlstein, 1996). And they seek these things not just for themselves but for their children as well. Few congregations have adopted Fox's ideas, and most gay men have probably not read about them.

Like the larger society, religious organizations are being forced to confront the gay issue. No longer are gay men and lesbians willing to live on the margin. They know their rights are being violated, and they are going to step forward and see that all social institutions change. The primary means of accomplishing this in the church seems to be to quietly show up and participate and give their gifts. As their fellows come to know them better, the oppression will become obvious, and the institution will change. This may not happen in five years or even in twenty. But the day will come when that change has been made, and people will look back at the common practices today in disbelief. Gay men and lesbians suffer from the current level of oppression, but their children may be the ones who suffer the most. Loving a father who is condemned weekly at religious services places the child in a bind. Gay fathers try to loosen this bind as much as they are able. One day they will have more help and understanding in their efforts to be the parents they want to be.

GAY GRANDPARENTS

Brad, a fifty-two-year-old widower, had defined himself as gay for years. He never came out to anyone, preferring the safe anonymity of clandestine meetings in parks with men he did not know. His wife had died ten years ago, about the time that his four kids were leaving home. His children and grandchildren are an important part of his life, and he also values the social status he has worked hard to achieve in his small Southern community. He "dates" a divorcee in order to fulfill his social obligation in a manner that does not arouse suspicion. Still on the sly, he has had a sexual relationship with a thirty-five-year-old man in the next town for the past two years. Brad recently tested positive for HIV.

I am in an absolute panic. My doctor tells me that I'm healthy and that I could go for years without having symptoms. But I notice every little bump on my skin, and every time I cough I think I have pneumonia. I have had no one to talk with about this. I am so ashamed of myself and shudder to think what people will say about me when I do get sick. I've thought about just saying I have cancer, but some of my friends are doctors, and they would ask me questions I couldn't answer. Imagine what Kay (my girlfriend) will think once she knows. Fortunately, we never had sex. I was too afraid that I might give her something, and besides, I was no longer interested in having sex with women. I made up a story that I had a very low sex drive and basically found myself no longer interested in sex. She has never pressed me about it, but I can see that she is more than a little puzzled. Mostly I date her because I am invited to lots of high-powered social events and need a companion who can mix with that social circle.

My real love is the young man I have been dating for almost three years. I know it sounds awful, but I am not willing to deny my gay side any longer, and I simply cannot give up my professional and social position. I finally talked with my boyfriend about what was going on. At first I thought he had given the virus to me, but it turned out that he was negative, so I guess I got it somewhere else. He tells me to sell my business, and he will come with me wherever I want to go. He thinks we can just leave everything behind.

I'm simply not willing to give up my children and my grandchildren. Last week, my four-year-old grandson spent the weekend with me. I had a great time taking him to the zoo and to the movies. Kay spent some time with us, but most of the time we hung around together. If my son even thought I had AIDS, he would probably not let me be around my grandson.

I've also thought about committing suicide when I begin to get sick. That's not the kind of thing I think I could do, but I also can't imagine what people will think of me when this gets out. They'll be talking about me for years, and even my friends will probably not want anything to do with me. I don't know what to do.

The other night at a dinner party someone was talking about how all the gays are getting AIDS. Kay told everyone that she thought they deserved whatever they got. Now what do you think she'll say when she finds out that her "boyfriend" is queer and has AIDS?

My counselor told me that maybe I should think about telling my children. He thinks they probably suspect that I am gay. Once when Tom (my boyfriend) was leaving, my daughter caught me kissing him goodnight. She just walked right out of the room, and nothing was ever said. I'm sure she told the others, but nobody has said anything to me. I suppose one of these days I'll have to tell them. God, I feel so bad about ruining their lives. They'll never get over this.

It also makes a mockery of my marriage. I valued the years we spent together. We had a great family life, traveling and watching our kids grow up. I still miss my wife. If she had lived, I probably wouldn't be in this mess. When she was around I behaved myself pretty well. I don't know what to do!

I thought about trying to do it in stages, and then I think about just blurting it out. First I would tell everyone that I was gay, and at least that would be over. But who would associate with me if they knew that about me? I don't know any gay people other than my boyfriend, and it's too late for me to start all that anyway. But if I do it that way, they would have time to adjust to my being gay, and then later I could tell them about AIDS.

I think people suspect that something is wrong with me. I've gained twenty pounds in the past six months. Just about all I do is go to work and sit around the house by myself and eat! I feel so safe at home alone, and I find myself turning down invitations for the first time in my life.

God, what am I going to do?

Gay grandfathers, like the gay community as a whole, are just now beginning to be more visible. As their children leave home and create their own families, once again these men encounter new questions about coming out. Will the partner be welcome at weddings? Who is going to tell the in-laws? How will the sons- and daughters-in-law feel about leaving children alone with them? As the children age, who is going to tell them? And how will their partners react to grandchildren being in the picture? One grandfather had this to say about engaging some of these questions:

My daughters knew I was gay when they got married. Thankfully (for them) I have been single, so there was not any tension about my bringing a partner at their weddings. I had asked them if they had told their fiancés about me before they married and was assured that they had. Still, there have been lots of awkward moments. One daughter just insisted that I go back in the closet when I come for a visit. She lives very near her husband's family, and visiting her also means visiting them. Over the years I became very frustrated with this situation, and I finally told her I would not come again until she had told them. I could tell she was in lots of distress over this, but one day she called and simply said, "All of us are looking forward to your being here at Christmas." It was only later that I learned she had not told them anything. When I confronted her about this she got very quiet and finally said, "Dad, I don't know how to do it."

She was right about that. The problem was that I was asking her to do something that was mine to do. So I wrote my son-in-law's parents and told them my story, ending the letter with a request that they let me know if they were uncomfortable and did not want me to come for a visit. A few days later I was given the green light to come on out. I have never had a conversation about it with them, and I know they do not approve. But they are the kind of people who would never create a scene, so I guess they deal with me the best they can. I still feel uneasy around them. They are fundamentalist Christians and belong to a religious organization that condemns homosexuality. Still, they are warm and polite to me. So mostly I just leave the topic out of my discussions.

These comments illustrate a common issue for gay grandparents: Whose responsibility is it to tell the new extended family and even the grandchildren about the grandfather's gayness? The problem is complicated by the difficulty in normalizing family conversations about the grandfather's sexual orientation. Although many gay men come out to their children, those who were formerly married report that they hesitate to bring up their gay social life with their children because they do not want to cause discomfort. Those who have not come out often comment that the whole family knows but that it is never discussed. These men need some help in learning to face the internal shame that often blocks them from initiating conversations with their children and other family members.

One thing is certain: in order for gay grandfathers and their grandchildren to maximize their relationship, effective communication must be in place. The grandparent and the parents will need to discuss when and how to tell the children. The grandfather must be prepared to deal with children who may be uneasy about allowing the grandchildren unlimited access with their grandfathers. The level of communication that would allow for effective resolution of issues like these is probably absent in many families. Research on gay grandparents does not exist today, so we must rely on anecdotal reports such as those in this chapter to understand this highly complex family behavior. Just as we are learning more and more about gay parenting, the day will come when we will know more about the needs of gay grandfathers and their grandchildren.

TIPS FOR PRACTITIONERS

As a human relations professional, you can add much to our understanding of the issues discussed in this chapter by writing about your work with gay fathers and their families. The suggestions that follow will help you know how to gather the understanding we need.

Provide Help for Once-Married Gay Fathers

It is usual for gay men who have been married to seek mental health services as they leave their families and begin lives in unfamiliar cultures. When appropriate it will be useful if you bring up the issue of children and dating relationships. You can aid the entire family by assisting the gay father in learning how to manage his emotions as he experiences the conflict between his children and his boyfriends. Your providing information about the stresses of dating on the children and the stresses of children on potential romantic relationships will help your client understand his need to develop effective communication skills. As communication improves, both children and boyfriends may have more positive attitudes about each other.

Learn About Local Religious Groups Who Welcome Gay Men

In larger cities, most people in the gay community are aware of churches and religious organizations that will welcome them. The challenges of finding spiritual support in smaller communities may be much more complex. By getting to know the local clergy's attitudes about gay men and gay parenting, you can serve as an invaluable consultant to gay fathers seeking religious affiliation.

Expand the Client's Awareness of the Difference Between Spirituality and Religion

Learning a model that can assist gay couples in understanding the difference between religion and spirituality will allow you to assist couples wherever they may be in their spiritual quest. "Resolving Spiritual and Religious Conflicts" and Figure 5.1, which appeared earlier in this chapter, describe a model that was developed for use with gay men who were dying of HIV disease; it will be useful in any discussion about spirituality and religion (Barret & Barzan, 1996).

Find Gay Grandfathers to Volunteer as Consultants

In almost every community there are gay men who are grandfathers. Seek them out and ask them to serve as consultants to other gay grandfathers who are trying to learn how to come out to their grandchildren. There are few visible models of how to handle this situation. Having someone who has been through it to consult with can be reassuring or might uncover unexpected pitfalls. It is important for you to interview these men first to be sure they are able and prepared to serve in this capacity.

Help Fathers Learn How to Disclose HIV Status to Their Children

Men like Brad need lots of support as they confront the very difficult issue of coming out as a father or grandfather with HIV disease. It is important to remember that when facing HIV disease, gay fathers suddenly may be hurled into a three-pronged dilemma: being a father, being gay, and having AIDS. Although treatments for HIV disease enable most of the infected to live reasonably normal lives, there is still no cure. The HIV-positive diagnosis and the progression of the disease more than likely will lead these men to disclose their homosexuality to spouses, children, and other family members.

Families dealing with the "triple whammy" may need more intensive help than other gay father families.

You must help families untangle these issues so that they can deal with them in a healthy and productive way. Unresolved issues related to the father's homosexuality and his fatherhood status also may surface for the first time because of the AIDS crisis. There is no "one best way" to handle this kind of situation. Some fathers will not come out to their children or grandchildren even as they approach death; others will share the information, allowing the family to move with greater understanding through any crises resulting from illnesses. As you discuss your client's decision, you will need to bring up the possibility that he may face rejection when he discloses his HIV status to his children.

6

Parents and Wives of Gay Fathers

One of the authors of this book tells about his experience in coming out to his wife, children, and mother when he was forty-seven. His decision to come out followed marital therapy focused on refreshing the relationship after his three daughters had entered adulthood. The dissolution of most marriages is complex and rarely is the result of one single factor. Realize that this change in his life only came after much reflection and many attempts to resolve other issues that threatened his marriage.

Telling myself I was gay was tough, but telling my wife and children was the absolute worst. I did not want to hurt them, but neither did I want to go on deceiving them. I had worried about my sexual orientation for most of my life, but I did not seem to fit the stereotype of the homosexuals I saw in the media. I figured I must not be gay since I could have sex with women. We married, and we had done a good job of supporting each other and our children. There was lots of affection between us, and we got along great most of the time. I kept asking myself why I could not continue like this for the rest of my life. Leaving would only be hurtful to me, and anyway I could see no way I would ever be able to live as an openly gay man. I was just too afraid.

All of that changed gradually. My kids were growing up and ready to leave home. My wife was busy with her career, and I knew that we needed to work out some of the issues between us as we headed into a new phase of our family life. So I was restless before I was confronted with an opportunity to look at my sexuality more closely. What happened was that I met some openly gay men in my profession, and as I watched them excel in their work and command respect from our coworkers, I suddenly saw that there was a way I could reclaim my integrity. Even though I had not had sex with men, I realized I needed to explore this side of me more fully. I could come out, continue in my work, and have a full and rich life. That realization came as a shock to me, and I decided to talk with my wife about it before I did anything else.

Telling her was so hard. I knew that what I was going to say would hurt her, scare her, and change forever the way we related to each other. But I also was determined to tell the truth—for once in my life not to deny myself. We went away for the weekend, and I began to talk with her about what was going on with me. I did not focus on her pain as I continued until I had told all of it. She listened and cried and became hysterical. The problem was that I did not know how to proceed. I was not ready to leave, and she did not want me to do that. Finally we agreed that I would begin to seek out nonsexual gay friends and see what happened. But you know, that was just a pipe dream. Not having sex was easy, but coming home to her distress was just about impossible. It took about four months for us to separate. The turning point came in a counseling session. I had been seeing a counselor since I came out to my wife. We talked a lot about my marriage and about my sexual feelings. As we talked about the marriage from the standpoint of the many issues that were between us, I began to see that I was compromising too much to be with a woman who was too dependent on me. Our marriage was in trouble because of issues other than my sexuality. I knew that regardless of my sexual orientation, we needed to separate.

By that time I did have friends in the gay community. Almost at once I knew I had come "home." The men I met were so much like me. We had so much in common, and for the first time in my life I felt like I could relax and be myself and not have to put up a front. I found the gay community welcoming, especially those men who had been married. They called, asked me to dinner, invited me to parties, and seemed genuinely concerned about my well-being. I could not have made it through those first few months without them.

My wife and I had agreed that neither of us would seek legal advice until a decision about the future of our marriage was made. But when I told her that I was leaving, she blew up and yelled, "I have seen a lawyer, and you are going to have to pay for being gay. I will get everything you have." I was stunned and angry that she had betrayed our agreement, and I let her know it. What was wrong in our marriage was not just my gayness, and I made sure she understood the many reasons I was leaving. Her threat to "take me to the cleaners" subsided as we talked, and we were able to work toward agreement on the main issues leading to separation. We made an appointment with an attorney and went to him with a property settlement already agreed on. I left the day before Thanksgiving and started a new life in an apartment with no phone and few furnishings. As bad as it was, I felt the "penalty box" I had chosen was deserved. That weekend was awful. I had no family around me, and my friends were not available.

We had also agreed that we would tell no one, especially the kids. My mother was in her late seventies, and I did not know what I was going to do about telling her. That got solved for me when she wrote me a letter that began, "At least your wife is honest about who she is. Why don't you just admit you are a homosexual?" I was flattened, and finally realized that my wife had told her. They had spent Christmas together (once again I had nowhere to go, but then I deserved more punishment, right?) and had always been close. Thus began my coming out to my family. I was not going to lie any longer. Once I had made that decision I knew what I wanted to do.

Those next few months were pretty awful. I was coming out to my kids, to the extended family, and to my coworkers. I was trying to figure out how to reinvent myself, struggling with feelings of shame and excitement. I felt like everyone I loved was angry with me. One of my friends kept encouraging me to come out of the penalty box. I had pretty much isolated myself, and sometimes I believed that the punishment I was experiencing was justified. Those who were around me were men I did not know very well. Accepting an invitation to spend a weekend at the beach to celebrate New Year's became a turning point for me. On New Year's Day we walked out on the beach, and I cringed at the sight of mothers and fathers and children playing in the surf. I was very self-conscious and worried about what they were thinking about me. One small boy stared at this group of men walking along and suddenly exclaimed, "Look, Mom, it's a bachelor party!" My immediate laughter at his comment went a long way toward reassuring me that I would be OK.

My mom did the best she could. She was seventy-seven when she learned that I am gay, and she lives in a very conservative community. We have been in the habit of exchanging letters all of my adult life. For the first couple of years after I came out I would cringe when I would see a letter from her. One might be very supportive and encouraging and the next would be angry and attacking. I came to call them her "grenades": some would blow up in my face, and some would be duds! I grew up in a family that was never close, and we don't see each other very often. Once I had talked with Mom about being gay, I told my brothers. I wanted them to hear it from me, and I wanted Mom to have others she could talk with about it. Actually my coming out opened up lots of dialogue between us.

Mostly that is the way it has been. Now, ten years later, my ex-wife and I are friends. A year after we split she wrote and thanked me for having the courage to leave. She knew that both of us were better off than we would have been had we stayed together. Now she has married a man who worships her, yet she still says appreciative things about the years we spent together. We get together a couple of times a year, and last Thanksgiving when my mom and all the kids were at my house, she joined us for a couple of days. I don't feel the need to be her best friend or even to keep up with her more regularly than we do. I hear about her through the kids, and we send cards back and forth on special occasions.

My mom and my brothers have also come around. Mom is not too interested in hearing about my life, and I have had to work hard to help her understand it. I don't think she has told any of her friends she has a gay son. I hate that I watch myself so closely when I'm around her. I don't want to rock the boat or cause her undue distress. She lives seven hundred miles away, and I think she is grateful for that distance. Recently I took her back to our hometown to visit the family cemetery. That was a good thing for us, and on the way home, for the first time, she asked how my "gay life" was going. She even said that she wished I were in a relationship. She does not like the idea of me being alone.

As afraid as I myself was of being alone, I can see that I have learned a lot by having to be more independent. I hope the day will come when I will be in a permanent loving relationship, but even if that does not happen, I am having a great time. The most startling thing about all of this has been that the part of me that I was so afraid of has become a gift. I would never have dreamed that I could be publicly gay and have so much loving support. I experience the gift when I am feeling comfortable with who I am, when I realize I no longer have to be afraid. And I see it when I tell nongay people about my community, and their stereotypes about gay men are refuted. I remember the day when I was driving to work, listening to music and negotiating the traffic. I suddenly was aware of a strange feeling that was unusual to me. As I sorted out the excitement I was feeling, I realized that I was happy! And *happy* is not a word many would have used to describe me before I came out. Out of all this pain and anguish I have become more confident, more at peace, and more in touch with the humorous side of my personality. I am one lucky guy to have such a rich and full life, one I would not have experienced had I remained in the closet.

Bob Barret
Charlotte, North Carolina

WIVES OF GAY FATHERS

The anecdotal reports from wives of gay fathers and indirect reports gathered from the gay fathers themselves indicate that at disclosure, most wives experience feelings of alienation from their husbands. A period of shock characterized by a sense of not really knowing the man with whom they have been so intimate masks a deeper level of concern that they are not able to trust their own perceptions of people around them (Strommen, 1989). Often they feel they have failed as wives and that perhaps their sexuality is also in question. Often the major concern is similar to that of parents: What did I do to cause him to become a homosexual? Although there may initially be anger, lingering hostility and bitterness rarely endure (Bozett, 1981a; Miller, 1979b; Ross, 1983). As noted previously, any conclusions we draw from this research must be tentative, because they rely on what are by and large retrospective data gathered from the gay fathers themselves, which may not be reliable.

Hatterer (1974) suggests that women who are married to gay men ignore the signals about their spouse's homosexuality as a way of staying in the maladaptive relationship that somehow meets their needs. These women play a deliberate but perhaps largely unconscious role in maintaining the facade of a traditional relationship. Many of the wives in another study were in highly dependent marital relationships that endured in spite of the obvious relationship deficiencies (Coleman, 1985). These women were afraid they would not be able to make it on their own and tended to focus on the positive aspects of their marriage, hoping that the unaddressed issues would disappear.

Gochros (1985) investigated the adjustment process of thirty-three women upon learning their husbands are gay. Their reactions were tied to the quality of the relationship, the timing of disclosure, and their attitudes toward homosexuality. As they struggled with shock, blame, and guilt, their general coping mechanisms either failed them or pulled them through. For example, those wives who were able to sort out confusing emotions and integrate new information in their responses to their husbands were more likely to adjust positively. Like other researchers, Gochros reports that most of the marriages ended in divorce.

Some wives seek a "cooling-off" period to give them time to digest this news. The reasons that couples remain married are very complex and rarely boil down to love and affection. Mothers may want to remain married for the sake of their children or because they are afraid to be alone or lack confidence that they can financially or emotionally cope with being a single parent. One wife of a gay father said,

> When Harry told me he was gay, I refused to believe him. We had good sex, and I could see no reason that he would think he was gay. I know that he went out alone from time to time, but I figured he was just hanging out with his friends. I really don't care if he is gay or not. I can give up sex with him. I just want him to stay with me and the kids. I don't think I could stand the humiliation of everyone knowing about him and maybe wondering about me. I need him here at home. He says he is not going to be having sex with men. I'm not sure I believe him. Mostly I just don't want to know what he is doing. We can work things out if he will just stay home.

Hays and Samuels (1989) reported on twenty-one women who were married to homosexual or bisexual men. The subjects in this study had anticipated a long-lasting monogamous relationship, and over half were separated or divorced, or reported themselves as being in transition following disclosure of their spouse's homosexuality. Three of the women in this study married with knowledge of their husband's sexual orientation. Common in their reports is the period of grief that accompanied disclosure, feelings of anger and betrayal over not having guessed the truth, and being blocked in seeking social support by their fears of disapproval and rejection. These fears were shared by their children and husbands. The three women in this study who were choosing to remain married to their homosexual husbands reported marriages characterized by good communication, knowledge of their husbands' sexual orientation, and an equal right to enter into sexual relationships outside the marriage.

One of the wives we interviewed stated,

> When Hal told me he was gay, I was absolutely stunned. I had thought he was having an affair with a woman because he was so reluctant to have sex with me. But I never thought he would be involved with men. I was ashamed and felt dirty and just wanted him to go away. I will never let him near my children again. He deceived me and does not deserve to be their father.
>
> I have never told any friend or family member what really happened between us. They wouldn't believe it and would probably not want to have anything to do with us after they knew the truth. I did rush to my doctor to have an AIDS test. So far I don't show any indication that I am infected, but I am afraid to get involved with anyone else. What kind of man would want me after knowing I was married to a queer and that I could have AIDS?
>
> When he said he wanted to see the kids, I just laughed and told him that they were gone from his life. If he tried to see them I would go to court and tell everyone about him. That shut him up for good.

Although such enduring anger and bitterness is not typically reported in the literature, some women do totally reject their husbands and use disclosure of homosexuality as a weapon in custody decisions.

Major questions about the wives of gay fathers remain to be answered. Among them are the following (Hays & Samuels, 1989, p. 83):

> Why do women enter heterogeneous marriages (heterosexual women married to bisexual or homosexual men), and are there

any special characteristics that differentiate these women from those who marry heterosexual men?

How do wives' experiences of such marriages differ during each stage, beginning with courtship, from experiences of wives married to heterosexual men?

Why do some women stay in heterogeneous marriages and others do not?

How do wives and children deal with the experiences and problems of disclosure, social stigma, and homosexual activities of the husband/father?

What special concerns do these mothers have for their children?

Are there differences in wives' experiences of the marriage based on the information provided or withheld before marriage about the husbands' sexual orientation and activities?

Do these wives experience major crises, and, if so, what factors precipitate them?

To whom do they turn for help?

It is clear that many women who have been married to gay and bisexual men have a difficult time finding validation and support for their experiences. In some cities, support groups are forming to allow these women to come together and share their situations. But in general these groups are few and far between, leaving most of these women alone. Likewise, there is scant literature for them to review that might help them gain perspective about their marriages. Although most of them report they eventually adjust to their life circumstances, there are no doubt countless others who do not come forward for assistance or who still remain in the dark about their husband's homosexuality. One woman said, "I suspect that my husband is sexually involved with men, but I'm afraid that if I bring it up, he will leave. I think I could live with this if I weren't so afraid

I might get AIDS. I don't know what to do. We haven't had sex in months; maybe he will just leave me alone."

Fortunately, a major investigation by Gochros (1989) provides some tentative direction for mental health professionals. Following up on her 1983 study, Gochros expanded her sample to include 103 women in several U.S. cities. The women were recruited from various sources, including publicity in newspapers, television, and radio, although they certainly were not representative of the general population. Largely white, middle class, and well educated, the participants nevertheless offered valuable information. These women were like women in heterosexual marriages. They lived fairly traditional lives, and many of them stayed with their husbands in spite of knowledge about their homosexuality. They reported their relationships in positive terms, and by and large were gay-positive. Those who remained in the marriage did so because either they were uncertain about what to do or because they experienced the relationship as mostly positive and had learned ways to cope with their spouse's gayness. This included meeting other gay men and learning about the gay subculture.

Gochros suggests that disclosure is best handled in the context of a loving relationship and includes in its content the expression of commitment to the wife. The wives in her study that made the best adjustment to disclosure had husbands who stated their love for their wives and children and who clearly saw their homosexuality as creating a dilemma for the family as a whole. They informed their wives directly of their situation and displayed empathy, concern, and reassurance to their spouses. For the wives in Gochros's study, the process of adjustment to disclosure involved three distinct phases:

1. The wife experienced an initial period of shock, which involved impaired intellectual and social functioning and was managed by attempts to stay calm and avoid impulsive actions.

2. An interim period, lasting from weeks to years, followed the first phase; this interim was dominated by confusion and anger.

3. Reintegration occurred once the family system adjusted to the change, found new resources, and learned new ways of defining individual needs and rights.

Whereas many of the women in the Gochros study (1989) sought help from family, peers, religious organizations, and often the mental health system, others isolated themselves and were extremely cautious about whom they informed. Unfortunately, their experience in getting help was much like that reported by gay men in that many of them found the professional sources to be misinformed and often insensitive. Most distressing were the mental health professionals who were punitive toward the wives and blamed them for the husband's problem. Some of the wives wished for mental health professionals who could endorse their staying married to a gay man as a viable alternative lifestyle. Even in cities as gay-positive as San Francisco, the quality of help available was frequently inadequate. More recent studies have corroborated the shock, anger, and reintegration of family members that Gochros (1989) describes in learning a family member is gay (Beeler & DiProva, 1999). Fear of their own rejection by society also has been documented as family members go through their own "coming out" to friends, coworkers, and neighbors (Crosbie-Burnett, Foster, Murray, & Bowen (1996).

COMING OUT TO PARENTS

Parents of gay fathers often face a dual crisis. If they have been unaware of their son's homosexuality, they encounter the emotions surrounding that information at the same time that they face their emotional responses to the potential dissolution of their son's family. Anxieties about the way his life will unfold, combined with renegotiating their relationship with their daughter-in-law and with concern for the well-being of their grandchildren, often leave these parents devastated and overwhelmed. Before we look at parental reactions to gay fathers, let's review some of the experiences related to coming out to parents. Some of the grief reactions parents face as they give up their sons' heterosexuality are listed in the next section. You will see that this process involves more than grief.

Fortunately, there has been significant research on the coming-out process. Virtually every book on the topic of homosexuality addresses the issues related to informing parents that one is gay. Parental responses fall along a continuum from total rejection to integration. Not unusual is one client's father's comment, "If you're gay, just don't come home again." That contrasts markedly with one mother's comment, "I've wondered if he was gay for years. It hurts me to think of the years he has struggled with this by himself. If only I had known, maybe I could have helped him not feel so alone and afraid. He is gay because he was born that way, and I admire his courage in living his life as the person he is." As is true about the adjustment to any change, accepting a son's homosexuality is a process that can take time.

Generally, gay men and their parents report that the initial reaction is negative. For parents, the news that a son is gay often conflicts with negative sanctioning about homosexual activity, and they tend to see their son's behavior as a choice. This is not surprising considering that "homosexuality refers to a type of behavior rather than a condition," and "homosexuals are viewed not just as people who do a certain type of thing, but rather as people who have a certain type of being" (Warren, 1980, p. 124). The son who had seemed so familiar suddenly appears as a stranger, and the parents encounter their own homophobia as well as their lack of knowledge about homosexuality. They are embarrassed and ashamed, and their attempts to encourage their son to abandon his gayness are often more connected to their own concerns about being stigmatized themselves. Their lack of knowledge renders them helpless as they attempt to find and construct a family role for a person who is homosexual.

Some gay men decide that telling their parents is not appropriate. Using the excuse that "it would just break their hearts," or "they're just too old to accept this," or "there's really no reason for them to know" cuts off parent and child from what can be both a painful and joyful aspect of their relationship. It also means that gay men will expend a certain amount of energy in keeping the secret, and excessive amounts of guilt might accumulate.

WHAT PARENTS SAY ABOUT GAY CHILDREN

Negative parental feelings are frequently followed by strong feelings of guilt and personal failure in the parenting roles (Weinberg, 1972; Jones, 1978). As parents of gay children begin to examine themselves, a usual question they ask is, "Where did we fail?" Although such feelings of self-blame are common, the research literature indicates that there is no basis for their legitimacy (Jones, 1978; Hooker, 1969; Newcomb, 1985; Zugar, 1980).

Stages of Parental Grief

Research suggests that as parents respond over time to the knowledge that their children are gay, they travel through five stages of mourning and loss, in the following order: shock, denial, guilt, anger, and acceptance (Robinson, Skeen, & Walters, 1987; Robinson, Walters, & Skeen, 1989; Skeen, Walters, & Robinson, 1988).

1. *Shock.* Parents said they were initially shocked when they discovered their child was homosexual. One mother said she was totally hysterical and spent two days in bed to recover. Feelings of disbelief and helplessness are also common. Their children had

suddenly become strangers, and parents feared the dangers of homosexual lifestyles. They worried that their children would want to have a sex-change operation, that their other children might also be gay, or that they had caused it; they worried because they didn't know anyone they could talk to. Other parents were simply concerned about covering up for their children to relatives, friends, and coworkers. Feelings of hurt, sadness, and depression often accompanied the shock or appeared as the shock wore off.

2. *Denial.* Once past the initial shock, parents typically tried to deny the reality that confronted them. They convinced themselves that this was just a phase their child was going through. "I thought it was not really true—that he would still meet someone from the opposite sex with whom he could have an intimate relationship," said one father. Another parent confessed, "I was unsure that it was so or that it was just something he was trying out—or copping out to."

3. *Guilt.* When the truth of their child's sexuality continued to confront parents, other emotions took over. "My feelings were intermixed and repeated over a period of two years," says a mother. "Because he asked us not to talk about it, it left us with a strand of hope for about a year. Then I knew I had to deal with it." Typical of most parents, this woman felt guilty and thought that she was to blame for her son's homosexuality. She said, "All I could think about was, Why us? What did we do wrong? I thought it was an illness caused by something I had done wrong or had failed to do that I should have done." Other parents felt guilty for harboring certain attitudes, like the father who confessed, "I felt that early prejudices and remarks were coming back to haunt me—that it was payback time." Another mother said, "I felt a little guilty about some attitudes—especially ignorance— that I had had about homosexuals."

4. *Anger.* Guilt and blame often naturally turned into anger directed toward self or spouse. "I was angry at my emotional reaction, angry at the pain it was causing my son," said one mother. The wife of a traveling salesman became furious with her husband for being

away from home so much. "See what you have caused," she retaliated frequently.

As parents became more informed about homosexuality, they learned that although its origins are unknown, they were not the cause of their child's homosexuality and that it is possible for homosexual men and women to lead happy lives. Still, this increased awareness sometimes was coupled with anger. Said one parent, "I began to talk more and to inform myself, mostly through reading. I felt he had a need to flaunt it, which I felt wasn't necessary. I don't feel that way now—I rather understand his need to be who he is without fear." Looking back, she reminisced, "It has been about nine years since I found out. I remember expressing anger, and I think I did it more because I thought I was supposed to react that way. At least it was a way of releasing feelings, and I had to do *something,* I thought." Another parent was upset that her son didn't trust her: "I was angry that my child didn't tell me sooner. I felt he didn't trust me enough to know I wouldn't reject him. I didn't understand his fears and trauma about coming out."

5. *Acceptance.* The journey from shock to acceptance corresponds to those stages experienced by people mourning the death of a loved one. In a way, this period of several months to several years can be thought of as a grief process for the death of their child's heterosexual identity—an identity these parents maintained since their child's birth. One man said he grieved for his son. "I mourned him as if he had died," he remembers. "I felt like he had died, even though intellectually I knew he was alive." And one woman said she felt grief for her own dreams for her child. Many parents described acceptance as a Dr. Jekyll–Mr. Hyde change. "I was relieved to at last really know my son," said one woman. "At least he would be his true self. The invisible wall had finally disappeared. No more living two different lives—one for himself and one for the family he loves. Now we could really relate—no more quiet dark places." Another parent, although upset to know what caused her son's unusual

behavior, was still relieved: "He told me on the phone, and when we finished talking and hung up, I cried and cried, and yet I was relieved to finally know for sure what was really wrong with him and what made him so depressed," she said.

Some parents become stalled in one stage of the mourning process and never completely worked through their reactions. "I felt like, and still do, that the joy has gone out of my life," confessed one mother. "I don't think I can ever be completely and totally happy again—not even for a moment." Some regressed on occasion to an earlier stage, like the father who said, "I still revert to denial," or the mother who said, "Denial, guilt, anger, and acceptance come and go from time to time, denial seldom and acceptance predominant."

In their book reporting the experiences of parents who have homosexual children, Griffin, Wirth, and Wirth (1986) validate the findings of the professional literature. Acknowledging the reality of the parents' pain and sorrow, joy, freedom, and commitment, they report that parents are distressed with religious attacks on homosexuals, that they often take on the responsibility for their child's homosexuality, and that they grieve the loss of grandchildren and status in their social networks. It is their loneliness that keeps them stuck, but in any case the movement to a positive viewpoint about homosexuality is not an easy one. Initially, the parents interviewed, who were participants in Parents and Friends of Lesbians and Gays (PFLAG), either broke off contact with their children, tried to convince them to change their sexual orientation, ignored the issue, or attempted to accept the reality of the situation.

Learning offers the best means to progress, and parents can find many sources of information: there are books that dispel many of the myths about homosexuality; other gay men and lesbians are available for dialogue; they can meet other parents of homosexuals through participation in a support group like those offered by PFLAG; they can seek out ministers and other clergy, although they must use some care in doing so; and there are professionals who can be extremely helpful in alleviating the all-too-common sense of alienation.

As parents confront their own homophobia and questions about their own sexuality, they must reformulate basic aspects of their worldview. Acceptance can come as they move from self-centered concern to empathy about their son's situation. As they recommit to their son and become aware of his pain, needs, and wants, they begin to reintegrate him into their lives. This usually means including his lover and other gay friends and may require that they become comfortable with physical expressions of closeness between men. Surprisingly, many parents find this son a source of strength as they come to appreciate the courage with which he is living his life and as they develop a more honest relationship with him. They often experience feelings of renewed pride, an ability to laugh about their situation, letting go, comfort in the ongoing relationship, and mutual expressions of love and affection. At this point some parents begin to "come out" themselves, either with information to only the extended family and friends or as activists for gay rights causes.

Robinson, Walters, and Skeen (1989) suggest that parents who find themselves absorbed with fear that their son will contract HIV should recognize that there is probably a connection between their feelings about this disease and the stigma attached to being homosexual. Magical thinking, such as "My child will be protected," is not going to be helpful. Rather, parents need to gather facts about HIV disease, discuss their concerns and share information with their son, devise an emergency plan in the event he does become infected, put their fears on hold, and communicate their trust to their son. Finally, parents are advised that drawing from the time they came to accept their son's homosexuality, they focus on accepting that they cannot change everything in their world and that they will survive better by being aware of the positive aspects of the relationship they have with their son. Some parents do get involved as volunteers in local AIDS service organizations and may find themselves reassured as they learn more about HIV disease and the variety of ways individuals and their families respond to it.

THE PROCESS OF PARENTAL ADJUSTMENT

The section "Stages of Parental Grief" provides a model of parental adjustment that focuses on grief. DeVine (1984) presents another five-step model that is different and may be useful for parents who do not see themselves as grieving. Each step has important issues demanding resolution, and not all families successfully move through all five steps; some become caught on one step indefinitely. According to DeVine, there is an initial time of *subliminal awareness* that their son or daughter is gay. These feelings are rarely discussed and often exist because of the parents' observations over the years. At disclosure or discovery, the *impact* of the news that these suspicions are true creates a crisis as the parents exert pressure on the child to change to a heterosexual orientation, and struggle with trying to keep this news secret. In this phase parents often feel alone and panicky.

The *adjustment* period comes as the parents gather information and learn that their child continues to demonstrate those qualities previously prized. Respect returns as the family begins to build a role for this member who is "different." During the *resolution* period, parents mourn the loss of their child's heterosexual role and its implication in terms of a lost family structure (for example, grandparenting) and changes in life, career, and social goals. As they mourn these losses, parents are also involved in dispelling the negative myths about the homosexual stereotype. Finally, there is a potential for *integration*, in which the new roles for all involved become more clearly defined, and new behaviors come to be seen as a source of growth for the family as a whole. DeVine sees this process as being heavily influenced by the degree of cohesion or closeness in the relationship and the degree of flexibility in the regulative structures, or rules and roles, that the family has created, and points out that the family members must renegotiate the family themes that define values and expected behaviors. Families that succeed in the process of integrating a homosexual member are likely to be those that prize differences and encourage individual expression, that use power flexibly, and that are able to see crisis as an opportunity for growth, not just as a danger. Those families with rigid rules and inflexible sex-role structures are likely to have a difficult time affirming a homosexual child (Storms, 1978).

Family themes often show up in subtle ways. One major theme is evident when parents struggle with the belief that their child can simply choose to be heterosexual, indicating that they are demonstrating a lack of knowledge about sexuality and homosexuality. Another theme is parents who exhibit shame and guilt and who may actually be struggling with ways to justify the incompatibility of their religious beliefs and homosexuality. Religion poses a unique challenge to these parents because often they have put great amounts of internal trust and social participation in religious institutions. Finding ways to affirm a child's homosexuality without abandoning what has been a major source of strength and meaning in their lives is an arduous, if not impossible, task for many.

Parents who are able to reformulate their old mind-sets are entering a time of changing their orientation both toward their own child and toward homosexuals in general. Those parents who can see that a homosexual lifestyle offers their child more than just a means of sexual expression are apt to move forward positively.

Now let's look at the particular reactions that parents have to gay fathers. As their son's marriage is dissolving and he discloses information about his sexuality that seems both horrendous and incompatible with his father role, the parents often join with the daughter-in-law and grandchildren in rejecting this former heterosexual whose behavior they thought they understood and could predict. The family as a whole is embarrassed and angry over what seems like an impossible situation. One mother wrote to her son, "I believe you are homosexual because you were born that way, but I don't see why you are choosing to be that now. Don't you love your children enough to keep on living the way you have for the past eighteen years?" A father said, "I guess I can accept him as a homosexual, but I just can't see why he would give up his family. Doesn't he know that they will not want him at their graduations and weddings and that he will never get to know his grandchildren? It seems like he expects all of us to just welcome him with open arms. It's just not going to be that way, especially since he obviously loves his boyfriends more than his children."

The reality is that having a gay son or father both adds and detracts from one's quality of life. On the one hand, there is a richness and diversity within the gay community that can become a source of tremendous satisfaction and enjoyment, and of course, learning about any minority group can enable people to give up limiting prejudices. On the other hand, just like their sons and fathers, parents and children of gay men will encounter stigma and rejection. In fact, many families do overcome these hurdles and find an incredibly rich, honest, and loving relationship with their sons, and they may acquire gay friends. When the gay father relationship can also include grandchildren, the family system as a whole is strengthened.

A final comment is necessary about the gay man who elects parenthood through adoption or by hiring a surrogate mother. Although not the norm, this form of fathering is an option that more and more gay men are choosing. Their parents, like the parents of any couple who choose such a means of having children, face a unique set of problems that require special attention. Often they struggle with their disapproval of their son's decision and may feel a particular burden as sole grandparents and as heterosexual models for their grandchildren. As courts become more open to approving adoptions by gay men, this option will become more available, and it is anticipated that some gay men will become fathers to children with HIV disease (Herscher, 1989). Never-married gay fathers have been virtually unstudied by researchers; what is known about them has been gathered through limited reports.

TIPS FOR PRACTITIONERS

If as a mental health professional you become involved with families of gay fathers, you will enhance your work by conceptualizing the emotional responses the family members present as emanating from a complex set of relationships and emotional interactions that are based in both the nuclear and extended family. It is also essential that you attribute the emotional responses to more than the fact that a husband, son, and father is acknowledging his homosexuality. We make suggestions here in the hope that your work with all family members will assist their successful integration of this change in the family constellation.

Help Family Members Deal with Self-Blame

All family members will toss around feelings of blame. Parents tend to struggle with guilt over having turned their son into a homosexual by faulty parenting. Wives may report feeling that their perceived sexual inadequacy drove their husbands to homosexuality. And the gay father, often feeling so totally responsible for the hurt and confusion he has created, may blame himself unfairly. Your proper stance is to provide information that will assist each person in understanding that homosexuality is not caused by anyone and to support the gay father's courage as he becomes more honest about who he is. You can steer family members away from wasting energy blaming themselves or others and toward examining their individual needs in light of this discovery; help the members of the family system find ways to offer each other mutual support. An important key in their healing is their identifying and confronting their anger and fear and dealing with these feelings in a constructive way.

Provide Information, Referrals, and Support Groups

You can be of service to some families by knowing religious figures in their communities who can provide sympathetic assistance as families wrestle with the clash between their values and their son's lifestyle. It is also helpful to be aware of other resources, both local and national, such as support groups for wives and parents, and literature that can help these individuals put their situation in better perspective. The most useful process will involve steps that alleviate the isolation that parents and wives report. Many family members come to understand and accept gay fathers with the support of PFLAG, which has chapters in every major city in the United States and the world. This organization provides emotional support and advice for parents and spouses who are struggling with a son's or husband's homosexuality.

Help Family Members Give Up Their Heterosexual Expectations

It is highly unlikely that the gay son or husband will change his sexual orientation back to a heterosexual lifestyle. It takes family members about two years to work through their grief and fully accept the gay father's same-sex orientation—the same amount of time it usually takes to complete the grief process associated with a divorce or death of a family member.

Borhek (1983) suggests that the grieving process serves the essential purpose of burying the old heterosexual image and creating a new homosexual image of the gay father. You can use approaches similar to those used in grief counseling to help family members come to terms with their feelings of loss over the death of the gay father's heterosexual identity. You can help family members understand that the longer they cling to the long-held fantasies of marriage, family, and a heterosexual lifestyle, the longer the mourning process takes. Once parents are able to bury their heterosexual expectations and accept their son's homosexual identity, parent-child bonds are strengthened and mothers and fathers report feeling closer to their children than ever before (Skeen, Walters, & Robinson, 1988).

Help Families Re-create Their Roles

By and large, reports indicate that disclosure is ultimately most helpful if it comes from the gay father in a context of a loving, ongoing relationship and if there is reassurance of a continued commitment. One mother's comment is typical: "When he told me he was gay, I thought he was also telling me good-bye. It was such a relief to know that he wanted to try to find ways for us to have a different relationship." Helping families create a role for the gay father is essential. Rather than allowing him to disappear, parents and wives can offer reassurance that he has a place in the family and that they are determined to help him work out that place. The system will need to change to accommodate his homosexuality and possibly his gay lover and friends. This too is a process that can take time, but it has the potential of being extremely rewarding to all.

The parent or ex-wife who initially rejected the gay father may seek help in reestablishing contact. Rather than having them wait around for the son or ex-husband to come to them, it will be helpful if they can begin to formulate an awareness of what they have to offer the relationship and what they need from it. Communicating these parameters to the gay father may enable him likewise to extend his trust back into a relationship with them.

Finally, there may be legitimate reasons for a gay father not to disclose his sexual orientation to his parents, former spouse, and children. In such cases, you can help him by encouraging him to explore the negative and positive consequences of his decision. This is best accomplished in an atmosphere that is not biased toward disclosure. Although obviously there are risks involved in nondisclosure (discovery, excessive guilt, and so on), there is no one way to handle the issue of coming out to family members.

7

Problems in Studying Gay Fathers

Claudia Flowers, Bob Barret, Bryan Robinson

Michael is an attorney who now lives in Portland, Oregon. We have been in touch with him over the past twenty years, as he has been a father to Kevin, who now lives in Asheville, North Carolina. Michael's willingness to continue his participation in our work allows for a rare glimpse of the life of a gay father over a twenty-year period.

Six months after my wife and I separated, I began to live together with Hunter, my first male partner, in a committed relationship. He was very fond of my five-year-old son and enjoyed caring for him. He frequently read him bedtime stories and helped in caring for him in other ways. My son's mother and I still made the major parenting decisions. For Hunter and me, those were happy months. We had alternate weeks to devote exclusively to each other, and we had supportive groups of friends, both straight and gay. We had been living together for six months when it became evident that, professionally, there was little future for either of us in the city where we lived. Furthermore, we wanted to live in an urban environment more receptive to our lifestyle. I was offered an excellent job opportunity in Washington, D.C. We decided that I should accept the job and that we would both move there. In considering the move, the question of how to maintain a shared role in parenting weighed heavily on my mind. I knew there was little chance of my former wife moving to

Washington. The only solution that she and I could agree on was for my son to fly to Washington every other weekend and spend most vacations there as well.

This arrangement left Kevin feeling abandoned and left me wanting to cram two weeks of parenting and love into alternate weekends. The move was disruptive for everyone. Hunter seemed unable to replace the supportive group of friends we left behind. We had more time together than ever before, but there seemed to be little focus to our relationship. At the beginning of the next school year, my former wife and son moved to Washington, and we resumed alternate weeks of parenting. Several months later, Hunter and I separated. My son expressed no feelings over this change. In fact, he delighted in being able to have my full attention! During the summers, my son spent much of his time with his grandparents. It wasn't until then that I felt comfortable dating other men. After the separation I worried about what signs of affection for another man would do to my relationship with my son. I was also afraid that my fitness as a parent might be brought into question by my former wife if there were signs of a new relationship.

During that summer I met Nick, my present partner. Our relationship had a chance to grow for several months prior to my son's return. We have been in a committed relationship now for a year and a half, although we have not lived together. On alternate weeks, the three of us are together several evenings, with Nick staying over those nights. I find myself trying to reinforce the bond of friendship and love between Kevin and me so that when he understands my sexual orientation, he will be able to draw on the strength of our relationship to weather what I anticipate may well be a difficult time. My greatest fear is that he will reject me and choose to live apart from me. This is the one fear that I think is unique to being a single gay father. I look forward to the day when this fear is history!

Michael
Portland, Oregon

A TEN-YEAR FOLLOW-UP OF
THE CASE OF MICHAEL

The first interview with Michael was conducted in 1980, when his son was seven years old—a time in his life when Michael worried if their relationship would endure his son's knowledge that his father is gay. We thought it would be interesting to contact Michael in January 1990 and ask him to give us an update.

In the ten years since my last interview, it seems that my life has now been through a complete cycle. Nick and I continued in our relationship for another year. With my attention constantly divided between Nick and my son, there seemed to be no balance possible in my life. As time went by, Nick and I grew further apart, and the relationship quietly ended. In a matter of months, I met Martin, who was eleven years my senior. Martin's twenty-year marriage was just ending. The fact that we both had children (Martin's were in college) gave us much in common. We quickly set up housekeeping and established the routine of a middle-aged married couple. With the apparent permanency of our relationship, my son became very jealous of Martin. He began to spend most of his time at his mother's house. I felt rejected and felt a great sense of loss. Through this experience, I began to admit the imbalance in my life and, as a result, entered therapy.

Among the issues to be dealt with was my progressive alcoholism. As I began to look at issues, my relationship with my son began to improve. With tremendous effort on Martin's part, he and my son formed their own relationship largely centered on their mutual love of football. They would spend long, boisterous hours in front of the television rooting for their favorite teams.

At the end of our third year together, I stopped drinking. Our fourth year I spent struggling with what seemed to be a forest of issues in my life. With the help of therapy and Alcoholics Anonymous I maintained my sobriety. The common denominator in my life seemed to be my need to please and take care of everyone but myself. I had very little self-esteem. The progress I made seemed to create distance between Martin and me. Much of what we had shared was based on our mutual negative life view. For me this had to change. Martin's unwillingness to make changes for himself resulted in my walking out of the relationship.

At about the same time, my son became the victim of physical abuse on the part of his stepfather. Because of this, he has chosen to live with me for the foreseeable future. We are both in therapy together and separately. We are trying to develop a healthy, honest relationship in which we are not codependent. My son is accepting of my being gay. I am open with him about my lifestyle, and I introduce him to the men I date. Some of his peers and their parents have been less accepting, so we are now more careful about sharing information.

For me to be the person (and the parent) I want to be, I must love, respect, and take care of myself. When this is happening, there is balance in my life. My son senses this, I know. As he matures, I see him as a more accepting and tolerant person than I am. He strongly senses the injustice surrounding gay-related issues, such as AIDS, as well as racial issues.

I look forward to the time when there is a significant man in my life again. However, for the next several years, I want to live separately from any lover I may have. I need to give this space to myself. Because of the healing in my own life, the fear of rejection by my son (and other significant people) is much less. I know that if rejection were to come, I would survive because I'm now learning to live with and love myself.

A TWENTY-YEAR POSTSCRIPT FROM MICHAEL

Ten more years have gone by. Kevin is now twenty-five and lives in the mountains of North Carolina. At fifty-seven, I am beginning a new chapter in my life with a new partner and a new job in a new city, Portland, Oregon.

The last ten years have been ones of tremendous growth for both Kevin and me. Shortly after my last writing, we learned that Kevin's various developmental problems and his awareness of constant suicidal "voices" were a result of brain damage sustained at birth. Despite treatment with various drugs, Kevin was constantly plagued by the disabling voices urging him to harm himself. It was a very traumatic period for us both.

In 1991, David, a very handsome Episcopal priest, walked into my life. He worked as a counselor in an AIDS hospice. David himself was diagnosed with the disease six months into our relationship. For the next two years, until David's death, I cared for him while simultaneously helping Kevin find a way of living with his disability.

We learned to live one day at a time. David taught me much about trust through his living with AIDS, and Kevin taught me much about determination and hope through his efforts to cope with his disability. As a result of ongoing participation in twelve-step recovery programs and the constant companionship of the shadow of death, in these ten years I learned much about living. Kevin too, not only through contending with suicidal tendencies but also through losing his best friend in a car accident, has had death as a teacher. We both have grown stronger through these experiences, with each of us finding our own spiritual path.

Today, though distance separates us, we are very close. We chat almost daily with the aid of the Internet. We share our lives and our love for each other openly and freely. When we visit in person there is wonderful warmth and sharing. Today the relationship is the best I could have ever dared hope for!

EMPIRICAL NEGLECT

Michael's case, which we followed for twenty years, is a good example of the kind of longitudinal self-report study that is needed for understanding gay fathers. What we know about these men, in fact, is very limited and is drawn almost entirely from self-reports from the fathers. A stronger, more scientific approach would enable the development of more efficient legal, social, and helping policies. This approach would involve large groups of gay fathers followed over a period of years during which they are given self-report inventories, interviewed, observed with their children and other family members, and even given standardized personality tests. The reasons this kind of research does not exist are many, as we discuss here.

Given that the role of fathering in general has been seen as a relatively unimportant factor in child development for generations, it is understandable that researchers would devote little attention to the experience of gay fathers. The prevailing belief was reflected in Margaret Mead's statement, "Fathers are a biological necessity but a social accident." This pervasive view supported the belief that the role of the father was unimportant in his offspring's development. Even though experts suggest that up to 25 percent of self-identified gay men father children (Harry, 1983; Miller, 1979a), the topic of gay fathers is perhaps the least discussed and researched area in the fatherhood spectrum. Recently, the role of fatherhood has begun to be researched more fully (Lamb, 1981, 1986, 1999; Robinson & Barret, 1986).

The fact that gay fatherhood is a sensitive area has further limited potential research activity. The social stigma surrounding the topic has resulted in sparse government-funded research and in many researchers avoiding this area for fear they will be labeled gay and their careers sabotaged. At some institutions, the topic of homosexuality is not considered a bona fide area of research for tenure and promotion.

In addition to these gay-negative conditions, other practical considerations have limited research activity in this area. The apparent incompatibility of being both gay and a father and the assumption of the negative belief that gay fathers do not exist have encouraged social science researchers to overlook this population. Further, the target population is difficult to reach, and obtaining representative samples is costly and time-consuming. Because of the inaccessibility of the target group, much of the gay father research takes the form of personal impressions or suffers from problems in sampling and research design. Another barrier is that many gay fathers do not participate in research studies for fear of becoming involved in custody disputes that might lead to curtailed visitation rights (Patterson & Redding, 1996). Thus the generalizations drawn must remain tentative and exploratory in nature.

Knowledge in social science is dependent on individuals volunteering to participate in research studies. Many gay fathers conceal their sexual identity due to fear of legal discrimination, violence, or both as a result of a backlash from the HIV-AIDS epidemic. Anxieties such as these are understandable, and we will continue to experience difficulty in recruiting research participants until society is more accepting of diverse lifestyles.

STATE OF THE RESEARCH ON GAY FATHERS

In the late 1970s, the two important research areas of homosexuality and fatherhood merged. The earliest accounts of gay fathers ranged from personal impressions (Carron, 1992; Mager, 1975; Voeller & Walters, 1978) to a handful of empirical investigations (Miller, 1978, 1979a, 1979b). Research on lesbian mothers also emerged at this time (Green, 1978; Hoeffer, 1981; Kirkpatrick, Smith, & Roy, 1981).

Our survey of the social science literature confirmed the limited research activities investigating gay fathers. A collection of empirical studies and their sample sizes, ages of participants, sample sources, locale of participants, data collection techniques, and methodology are listed in Table 7.1. The research studies listed are not an exhaustive collection of empirical research on gay fathers

Table 7.1. Demographic and Methodological Characteristics of Selected Gay Father Research

Study	Sample Size	Age	Sample Source	Locale	Data Collection	Methodology
Bigner & Jacobsen, 1992	24 gay fathers, 29 gay men	M = 41.5	Support group	West	Standardized instruments	Comparative study
Bozett, 1980, 1981a, 1981b	18	R = 28–51	Support group	West	Interviews	Grounded theory
Crosbie-Burnett & Helmbrecht, 1993	48 stepfamilies	R = 35–46	Advertising and clinical referrals	National (large cities)	Standardized instrument	Descriptive
Dunne, 1987	7	M = 43	Support group	Northeast	Clinical observations	Qualitative
Harris & Turner, 1986	10	M = 37	Support group	West	Questionnaires	Comparative study
Miller, 1978, 1979a, 1979b	40	R = 24–64	Snowball	Cross-national (United States) and Canada	Interviews	Life history
Skeen & Robinson, 1984	30	M = 41.4	Support group	National	Questionnaires	Descriptive
Turner, Scadden, & Harris, 1990	10	M = 37	Support group	West	Questionnaires	Comparative study
Wyers, 1987	32	M = 40.1	Advertising	Northwest	Interviews	Comparative study

Note: M = mean, R = range

but represent the types of empirical research used to investigate gay fathers. You may wish to refer to other references for a more comprehensive review of research findings (see Barret & Robinson, 1990, 1994; Bigner & Bozett, 1990; Bozett, 1989, 1993; Patterson & Chan, 1996, 1999).

Research Paradigms

Two research paradigms have been used in the study of gay fathers, qualitative and quantitative. Early researchers of gay fathers used qualitative research methodology to examine gay fathers (for example, the Bozett and Miller studies). Qualitative methods are constructivist approaches in which inductive logic prevails; that is, the theories are derived from observations. This methodology provides a rich description of gay fathers and is invaluable in providing initial information and allowing for theory development. One limitation of qualitative research methods is the lack of generalizability of the results; in other words, the research findings apply to the sample of subjects in the research study but may not apply to gay fathers who were not involved in the study. Generalizability of results is referred to as external validity of research and is better achieved using quantitative research methods.

In quantitative research, information about the gay father is gathered from samples. Two important sample characteristics are needed for generalizing the results to a target population: adequate sample sizes and samples that accurately represent the population. The larger the sample size, the more confident we can be that the findings have captured the characteristics of the population of gay fathers. As Table 7.1 indicates, sample sizes of these and other studies are too small to place a great deal of confidence in the findings.

Obtaining representative samples in social science research is difficult, and research in sensitive areas where little is known about the target population compounds the difficulty. In research on gay fathers, the men studied tend to be in their forties, white, and middle class. Most of the studies are concentrated in large cities in the

western United States, each with its own distinct regional characteristics. Such cities as San Francisco, Seattle, and Denver are over-
represented in this body of literature and contain higher gay
populations where research subjects are more accessible. These
urban areas are also known for more liberal attitudes and lifestyles
than is the case in many other areas in the country. In addition,
most of the samples were drawn from support groups or recruited
from advertising. Fathers in gay support groups, already clustered
together for a common purpose, are likely to be different from fathers who do not belong to groups or from gay fathers within the
group who did not return their questionnaires. The gay parents who
participated in the research have identified publicly as gay, whereas
gay parents who maintain privacy are difficult to identify and may
have different characteristics from those fathers willing to participate in research studies. Thus the generalizations drawn must remain tentative and exploratory in nature.

The Use of Self-Report Data

The results of any empirical study are only as good as the validity
or accuracy of the outcome measures used in the study. Most of the
studies on gay fathers employ self-report data, either through mailed
questionnaires or face-to-face interviews. This means that practically everything we know about gay fathers is what these men told
us. The entire body of findings rests on the self-reports of men who
volunteer to come forth. This is perhaps the most serious problem
of all, because what respondents say they feel or believe does not
necessarily match their actual behaviors. Moreover, one motivation
for gay fathers to participate may be to present themselves in a more
favorable light in order to counter discrimination and victimization.
Harris and Turner (1986), for example, noted that in their study,
"The gay parents may have been particularly biased toward em-
phasizing the positive aspects of their relationships with their children, feeling that the results might have implications for custody
decisions in the future" (p. 111). This tendency to unwittingly slant

responses to produce favorable outcomes is a limitation in all social science research that is dependent on self-report. Most research participants want to present themselves in a socially desirable light.

Many of the quantitative studies compare the differences between gay fathers and gay men without children, heterosexual fathers, or lesbian mothers. This research design assumes that all gay fathers are homogeneous or alike. We know that there is diversity among gay fathers (for example, divorced custodial fathers, divorced noncustodial fathers, fathers of adopted children, gay fathers with a partner, and gay fathers without a partner). Examining diversities among gay fathers can provide rich information concerning the quality of types of parenting arrangements. A good example of a study that looks at the diversity among gay fathers is that of Crosbie-Burnett and Helmbrecht (1993), which predicted what factors contributed to the happiness of gay stepfamilies.

The profile we use to understand and describe gay fathers is far from conclusive. Clearly, since 1982 the literature has improved in the use of comparison groups and a more diverse, nationwide sampling. This is not meant to criticize the earlier studies, for they were pioneers of research on gay fathers and provided the impetus for future studies. Still, until researchers can obtain larger, more representative samples that employ more sophisticated research designs, one must be cautious in making sweeping generalizations about gay fathers. Meanwhile, it is possible to make only limited speculations from some indirect sources and from a handful of direct sources that pave the way for future inquiry.

STATE OF THE RESEARCH ON CHILDREN OF GAY FATHERS

Research on children of gay fathers is even sparser than that on gay fathers. In addition to the factors that contribute to limited research activities on gay fathers, today's research ethics and sensitive social scientists are more protective of children. The problems with the research studies investigating children of gay fathers are similar to the problems encountered in studying gay fathers themselves; that is, the results are based on small, nonrepresentative samples, and data are collected using subjective self-report.

Many of the conclusions about the development of children of gay parents have been based on studies of lesbian mothers. Although information gained from these studies is useful, generalizing from these studies could provide incorrect information concerning children of gay fathers. We know from existing findings that lesbian mothers have significantly lower incomes than gay fathers, are less likely to live with a lover, are more likely to tell their children about their homosexuality, and are more likely to have trouble reconciling their gay and parenting roles (Turner, Scadden, & Harris, 1990). These differences could account for different developmental outcomes among the offspring of gay men.

There is virtually no information on the developmental outcomes of young children living in gay father households. The body of research on the children of gay fathers is woefully incomplete and for the most part relies heavily on data from lesbian mothers and their children. Although we know that the sexuality of children of gay fathers is not influenced by their parents' sexual orientation and that these children are sexually abused no more than children from heterosexual homes, many important questions remain, and new theoretical models need to be developed. Long-term studies on the psychological and social impact of living with a gay father need to be conducted in relation to the child's self-concept and social relationships with peers. We need to know the positive and negative aspects for children reared in two worlds—one gay and one straight. We need to know ways in which children cope with the stigmatizing nature of their gay father's sexuality, and we need to know what kind of home environment fosters positive child development.

Previous theory in child development assumed that a child is healthier when raised by a heterosexual couple. The research findings with lesbian mothers and gay fathers have challenged these child development theories. Family structure is not the critical issue in raising healthy children, but evidence now suggests that family processes and interactions are better predictors of a child's health (Patterson & Chan, 1999). These findings suggest that carefully constructed research questions need to be developed and empirically tested.

SUGGESTIONS FOR
FUTURE RESEARCH

All social science research has flaws, and the results are tentative, but this does not give us license to continue producing research with conceptual and methodological flaws. Much research needs to be done in the area of gay fathers and child development. Researchers need to examine many unanswered questions and develop new theoretical concepts. The previous research has been helpful for dispelling myths about gay fathers and questioning the old theories of child development; however, methodological and conceptual issues need to be addressed.

The sampling and methodological flaws previously discussed are common in most social science research. Studies examining human behavior are very complex, and investigations into sensitive areas only add to the research complexity. But this does not mean that we should fail to strive for better research methodology and procedures. As long as research studies on gay fathers are riddled with procedural problems, the findings will be questioned. Lack of rigorous research provides ammunition for critics to continue to wield homophobic attitudes, victimize the target population, and refute current findings. It is essential to develop more sophisticated research inquiries that will lend credence to gay fatherhood as a legitimate area of study and a viable parenting style.

Procedures for obtaining samples of gay fathers that represent the overall population of gay fathers are essential for generalizing results. The first step in obtaining representative samples is to have a detailed description of the population being studied. As long as our society continues to discriminate against gay men, describing this population will be difficult. Still, there are some techniques that will ensure that our samples have more diverse representation. For example, stratified sampling techniques could be used to ensure that the sample has representation from different parts of the country or world and diverse ethnic makeup, socioeconomic status, and family structure. This will help ensure that we do not continue to investigate only white, well-educated, Western gay fathers. Reliance on unrepresentative samples of gay fathers in one exclusive urban area will not provide a complete picture of the gay father experience. Selection of subjects should be based on the aforementioned diversity.

Sample size must be increased. Larger sample sizes have a greater chance of capturing the target population's characteristics. In addition, larger sample sizes increase the statistical power for detecting differences between groups in comparative studies. The use of small samples allows critics to argue that no differences between groups were found, citing inadequate statistical power. The size of the samples needed for a particular study should be estimated using a power analysis that would provide the researcher with sample size requirements for their particular research question.

Questionnaires and interviews are valuable tools for information gathering but have many limitations. Methods for reducing the socially desirable responses together with methods for cross-checking of the data would significantly improve the quality of the data. An example of cross-checking data can be found in the study by Bailey, Bobrow, Wolfe, and Mikach (1995). When examining the sexual orientation of the sons of gay fathers, these researchers obtained information not only from the sons but also from the fathers, which allowed the researchers to check for consistency in the data. In addition, researchers need to use other methods and tools for collecting information. For example, data collection methods using observations and standardized instruments would not rely as heavily on research participants' perceptions.

Many of the research questions on gay fathers provide a simplistic model for investigation. Most of the research to date has been analyzed at the father or child level. The father and child do not live in isolation and are affected by many aspects of their lives. It is essential that future researchers employ a systems-oriented approach and assess perceptions and behaviors of spouses, fathers, children, grandparents, and significant others in the gay father's life. Examining the interactions within the family and community requires multilevel analyses.

When information is collected from research participants, it is important that this information accurately model reality. This requires that researchers collect multiple outcomes in which most outcomes have multiple causes and in which most causes have multiple effects (Thompson, 1986). For interactions between outcomes and causes to be understood, a full network of all possible relationships must be considered simultaneously within the analysis. This requires sophisticated modeling and multivariate data analyses. These models will provide a more realistic picture of gay fathers and their offspring.

Basic research is guided by theory, and research questions are then derived from that theory. The research question serves as the guide for the empirical research study. Most of the empirical studies of gay fathers attempt to describe gay fathers or examine the myths that surround gay fathers (as described in Chapter Two). These myths have been dispelled by empirical research. Although these research questions are important for informing the judicial process, they are in themselves homophobic; that is, they assume the myths about gay fathers are true.

Developmental studies are essential for understanding the different stages of gay fatherhood. Research methods, such as longitudinal and cross-sectional studies, need to be conducted. More men like Michael are needed to give us a more complete understanding of gay fathering across the life span. Developmental studies of gay fathers are essential for understanding the different stages of gay fatherhood and assessing attitudinal and behavioral differences over time. Future investigations should also address the kinds of long-term adjustments and adaptations that gay fathers make, or need to make. Those participants who are first-time fathers in young adult-hood and who lose contact with mother and baby can be studied later, as older men, to measure potential psychological aftereffects.

TIPS FOR PRACTITIONERS

Social workers, teachers, family counselors, and the clergy must continue to explore alternatives to Freudian theory, which emphasizes pathological behavior. Although researchers have made efforts to move beyond Freudian theory, much work remains to be done. Clearly, antiquated Freudian themes continue to dominate the thinking of many practitioners. Simplistic Freudian explanations from the turn of the century will not work in our complex society, and speculation needs to be replaced with knowledge.

You can disseminate nonprejudicial information to the general public by writing for the popular press or speaking in public forums. Contact with legislators at both local and national levels would also be a catalyst for changes in attitude. The helping profession can co-operate, within legal and ethical confidentiality constraints, with research on gay fatherhood. Funding agencies, social agencies, and researchers can combine their resources to improve the information base concerning gay fathers. Funding agencies can also be more sensitive to the many obstacles that researchers encounter in attempting to gather meaningful information. Health clinics, residential homes for children, hospitals, public schools, day-care centers, and other human service agencies that have gay parents as clients can cooperate with research efforts. Social agencies can also be more co-operative with researchers. It is important for agencies to protect their clients from exploitation. Well-developed research activities conducted by ethical professionals, however, can help erase common myths and homophobic attitudes and ultimately can improve the nature and quality of medical, legal, custodial, and other human services rendered to gay fathers.

Appendix

Internet Resources

The following Web pages include abundant information on gay fathering. We have chosen these because they are posted by organizations that have both a history (the address is unlikely to change) and a reputation for excellence (information is likely to remain current). Each of these pages contains links to other websites that will contain valuable information.

American Psychological Association

http://www.apa.org/pi/l&bres.html
http://www.apa.org/pi/preface.html
http://www.apa.org/divisions/div44/

American Counseling Association

http://www.aglbic.org/resources/rt07.htm

Gay Fathering Pages

http://www.gaydads.com/
http://ucl.broward.cc.fl.us/pathfinders/lsbgayprt.htm
http://www.familypride.org
http://userwww.service.emory.edu/~librpj/gaydads.html
http://home.swbell.net/dennisf/gamma/gamma.htm
http://www.adlbooks.com/parent.html
www.milepost1.com/~gaydad/TOC.html

Adoption

http://news.mpr.org/features/199711/20_smiths_fertility/part6/index.
html
http://www.adoptive.com/
http://www.adoptme.com/gay.htm
http://www.adopt.org/datacenter/faces/articles/gay/gay3.html
http://www.growthhouse.org/gayfams.html

Lambda Legal Defense and Education Fund

http://lldef.org/cgi-bin/pages/search

Children and Parents of Gay Fathers

http://www.colage.org
http://www.pflag.org

References

APA (1997). Resolution on appropriate responses to sexual orientation. www.apa.org/pi/resglbc.html

Alexander, M. B., & Preston, J. (1996). We were baptized too: Claiming God's grace for lesbians and gays. Louisville, KY: Westminster John Knox Press.

American Psychiatric Association. (1974). Position statement on homosexuality and civil rights. *American Journal of Psychiatry, 131*, 497.

Bailey, J., Bobrow, D., Wolfe, M., & Mikach, S. (1995). Sexual orientation of adult sons of gay fathers. *Developmental Psychology, 31*, 124–129.

Baptiste, D. A. (1987). Psychotherapy with gay/lesbian couples and their children in "stepfamilies": A challenge for marriage and family therapists. *Journal of Homosexuality, 14*, 223–238.

Baptiste, D. A. (1988). Psychotherapy with gay and lesbian couples and their children living in stepfamilies: A challenge for marriage and family therapists. In E. Coleman (Ed.), *Integrated identity for gay men and lesbians: Psychotherapeutic approaches for emotional well-being* (pp. 223–238). Binghamton, NY: Harrington Park Press.

Barbone, S., & Rice, S. (1994). Coming out, being out, and acts of virtue. *Journal of Homosexuality, 27*, 91–110.

Baron, J. (1996). Some issues in psychotherapy with gay or lesbian clients. *Psychotherapy, 33*, 611–616.

Barret, B. (1998). Gay and lesbian activism: A frontier for social action. In C. Lee & G. Walz (Eds.), *Social action: A mandate for counselors* (pp. 83–98). Washington, DC: American Counseling Association.

Barret, B., & Barzan, B. (1996). Spiritual experiences of gay men and lesbians. *Counseling and Values, 41*, 4–15.

Barret, B., & Barzan, B. (1997). Gay and lesbian spirituality: A response to Donaldson. *Counseling and Values, 42*, 222–224.

Barret, R. L., & Robinson, B. E. (1990). *Gay fathers*. San Francisco: New Lexington Press.

Barret, R. L., & Robinson, B. E. (1994). Gay dads. In A. E. Gottfried & A. W. Gottfried (Eds.), *Redefining families: Implications for children's development* (pp. 157–170). New York: Plenum.

Barts, M. (1999, February). Rising number of single fathers reflects changing attitudes in society. *Counseling Today*, 15–16.

Barzan, R. (1995). *Sex and spirit: Exploring gay men's spirituality*. San Francisco: White Crane Press.

Beane, J. (1981). "I'd rather be dead than gay": Counseling gay men who are coming out. *Personnel and Guidance Journal*, 60, 222–226.

Beeler, J., & DiProva, V. (1999). Family adjustment following disclosure of homosexuality by a member: Themes discerned in narrative accounts. *Journal of Marital and Family Therapy*, 25, 443–459.

Bell, A. P., & Weinberg, M. S. (1978). *Homosexualities: A study of diversity among men and women*. New York: Simon & Schuster.

Bell, A. P., Weinberg, M. S., & Hammersmith, S. K. (1981). *Sexual preference: Its development in men and women*. Bloomington: Indiana University Press.

Bem, S. L. (1974). The measurement of psychological androgyny. *Journal of Consulting and Clinical Psychology*, 42, 155–162.

Ben-Ari, A. (1995). Coming out: A dialectic of intimacy and privacy. *Families in Society: The Journal of Contemporary Human Services*, 76, 306–314.

Bieber, I. (1962). *Homosexuality: A psychoanalytic study*. New York: Basic Books.

Bigner, J. J., & Bozett, F. W. (1990). Parenting by gay fathers. In F. W. Bozett & M. B. Sussman (Eds.), *Homosexuality and family relations* (pp. 155–176). Binghamton, NY: Harrington Park Press.

Bigner, J. J., & Jacobsen, R. B. (1989a). Parenting behaviors of homosexual and heterosexual fathers. *Journal of Homosexuality*, 18, 173–186.

Bigner, J. J., & Jacobsen, R. B. (1989b). The value of children to gay and heterosexual fathers. *Journal of Homosexuality*, 18, 167–172.

Bigner, J. J., & Jacobsen, R. B. (1992). Adult responses to child behavior and attitudes toward fathering: Gay and nongay fathers. *Journal of Homosexuality*, 23, 99–112.

Borhek, M. (1983). *Coming out to parents: A survival guide for lesbians and gay men and their parents*. New York: Pilgrim Press.

Bozett, F. W. (1980). Gay fathers: How and why they disclose their homosexuality to their children. *Family Relations: Journal of Applied Family and Child Studies*, 29, 173–179.

Bozett, F. W. (1981a). Gay fathers: Evolution of the gay-father identity. *American Journal of Orthopsychiatry, 51*, 552–559.

Bozett, F. W. (1981b). Gay fathers: Identity conflict resolution through integrative sanctioning. *Alternative Lifestyles, 4*, 90–107.

Bozett, F. W. (1982). Heterogeneous couples in heterosexual marriages: Gay men and straight women. *Journal of Marital and Family Therapy, 8*, 81–89.

Bozett, F. W. (1983, October). *Gay fathers: Social policy concerns*. Paper presented at the annual meeting of the National Council on Family Relations, Washington, DC.

Bozett, F. W. (1984a, October). *The children of gay fathers: Strategies for coping with identity variance*. Paper submitted at the National Council on Family Relations, San Francisco, CA.

Bozett, F. W. (1984b). Parenting concerns of gay fathers. *Topics in Clinical Nursing, 6*, 60–71.

Bozett, F. W. (1987). *Gay and lesbian parents*. New York: Praeger.

Bozett, F. W. (1988). Social control of identity by children of gay fathers. *Western Journal of Nursing Research, 10*, 550–565.

Bozett, F. W. (1989). Gay fathers: A review of the literature. In F. W. Bozett (Ed.), *Homosexuality and the family* (pp. 137–162). Binghamton, NY: Harrington Park Press.

Bozett, F. W. (1993). Gay fathers: A review of the literature. In L. Garnets & D. Kimmel (Eds.), *Psychological perspectives on lesbian and gay male experiences* (pp. 437–457). New York: Columbia University Press.

Bryant, A. S., & Demian, R. (1994). Relationship characteristics of American gay and lesbian couples: Findings from a national survey. In L. A. Kurdek (Ed.), *Social services for gay and lesbian couples* (pp. 101–117). New York: Haworth Press.

Campbell, K. (1994, November 18). A gay father's quiet battle. *Washington Blade*, p. 5.

Carron, J. (1992). On being a gay father. In B. Berzon (Ed.), *Positively gay: New approaches to gay and lesbian life* (pp. 102–110). Berkeley, CA: Celestial Arts.

Chekola, M. (1994). Outing, truthtelling, and the shame of the closet. *Journal of Homosexuality, 27*, 67–90.

Coleman, E. (1985). Integration of male bisexuality and marriage. *Journal of Homosexuality, 11*, 189–207.

Collins, L., & Zimmerman, N. (1983). Homosexual and bisexual issues. In J. C. Hansen, J. D. Woody, & R. H. Woody (Eds.), *Sexual issues in family therapy* (pp. 82–100). Rockville, MD: Aspen Publications.

Comstock, G. (1996). *Unrepentant, self-affirming, practicing: Lesbian, gay and bisexual people within organized religion.* New York: Continuum.

Cramer, D. (1986). Gay parents and their children: A review of research and practical implications. *Journal of Counseling and Development, 8,* 504–507.

Crosbie-Burnett, M., & Helmbrecht, L. (1993). A descriptive empirical study of gay male stepfamilies. *Family Relations, 42,* 256–262.

Crosbie-Burnett, M., Foster, J., Murray, C., & Bowen, G. (1996). Gays' and lesbians' families-of-origin: A social-cognitive-behavioral model of adjustment. *Family Relations, 45,* 397–403.

Dank, B. M. (1972). Coming out in the gay world. *Psychiatry, 34,* 180–197.

D'Augelli, A. R. (1992). Teaching lesbian and gay development: From oppression to exceptionality. *Journal of Homosexuality, 22,* 213–227.

Decker, B. (1984). Counseling for gay and lesbian couples. *Practice Digest, 7*(1), 13–15.

DeFrancis, V. (1976). *Protecting the child victim of sex crimes committed by adults.* Denver: American Humane Society, Children's Division.

DeVine, J. L. (1984). A systematic inspection of affectional preference orientation and the family of origin. *Journal of Social Work and Human Sexuality, 2,* 9–17.

Drucker, J. (1998). *Families of value: Gay and lesbian parents and their children speak out.* New York: Insight Books.

Dunne, E. J. (1987). Helping gay fathers come out to their children. *Journal of Homosexuality, 13,* 213–222.

Eger, D. (1992). Judaism: A time of change. In B. Berzon (Ed.), *Positively gay: New approaches to gay and lesbian life* (pp. 133–141). Berkeley, CA: Celestial Arts.

Einstein, E. (1982). *The step family: Living, loving, and learning.* Old Tappan, NJ: Macmillan.

Epstein, R. (1979, June). Children of gays. *Christopher Street,* 43–50.

Fadiman, A. (1983). The double closet. *Life Magazine, 6,* 76–100.

Fassinger, R. E. (1991). The hidden minority: Issues and challenges in working with lesbians and gay men. *Counseling Psychologist, 19,* 151–176.

Fox, M. (1984). The spiritual journey of the homosexual . . . and just about everyone else. In R. Nugent (Ed.), *A challenge to love: Gay and lesbian Catholics in the church* (pp. 189–204). New York: Crossroads.

Gagnon, J., Laumann, E., Michael, R., & Michaels, S. (1994). *The social organization of sexuality.* Chicago: University of Chicago Press.

Gallup, G. (1977). *The Gallup opinion index* (Report no. 147). Princeton, NJ: American Institute of Public Opinion.

Garnets, L., Hancock, K., Cochran, S., Goodchilds, J., & Peplau, L. (1991). Issues in psychotherapy with lesbians and gay men: A survey of psychologists. *American Psychologist, 46,* 964–972.

Gebhard, P., Gagnon, J., Pomeroy, W., & Christenson, C. (1965). *Sex offenders: An analysis of types.* New York: HarperCollins.

Geiser, R. L. (1979). *Hidden victims: The sexual abuse of children.* Boston: Beacon Press.

Gochros, J. S. (1985). Wives' reactions to learning that their husbands are bisexual. *Journal of Homosexuality, 11,* 101–113.

Gochros, J. S. (1989). *When husbands come out of the closet.* Binghamton, NY: Harrington Park Press.

Goffman, E. (1963). *Stigma.* Englewood Cliffs, NJ: Prentice Hall.

Golombok, S., & Tasker, F. (1994). Children in lesbian and gay families: Theories and evidence. *Annual Review of Sex Research, 5,* 73–100.

Gomes, P. J. (1996). *The good book: Reading the Bible with mind and heart.* New York: Avon Books.

Goss, R. (1993). *Jesus acted up: A gay and lesbian manifesto.* San Francisco: Harper San Francisco.

Green, G. D., & Bozett, F. W. (1991). Lesbian mothers and gay fathers. In J. C. Gonsirek & J. C. Weinrich (Eds.), *Homosexuality: Research implications for public policy* (pp. 197–214). Thousand Oaks, CA: Sage.

Green, R. (1978). Sexual identity of thirty-seven children raised by homosexual or transsexual parents. *American Journal of Psychiatry, 135,* 692–697.

Griffin, C. W., Wirth, M. J., & Wirth, A. G. (1986). *Beyond acceptance: Parents of lesbians and gays talk about their experiences.* Englewood Cliffs, NJ: Prentice Hall.

Groth, N., & Birnbaum, J. (1978). Adult sexual orientation and attraction to underage persons. *Archives of Sexual Behavior, 7,* 175–181.

Harris, M. B., & Turner, P. H. (1986). Gay and lesbian parents. *Journal of Homosexuality, 12,* 101–113.

Harry, J. (1983). Gay male and lesbian relationships. In E. D. Macklin & R. H. Rubin (Eds.), *Contemporary families and alternative lifestyles* (pp. 216–234). Thousand Oaks, CA: Sage.

Hatterer, M. S. (1974). The problems of women married to homosexual men. *American Journal of Psychiatry, 131,* 275–278.

Hays, D., & Samuels, A. (1989). Heterosexual women's perceptions of their marriages to bisexual or homosexual men. *Journal of Homosexuality, 18,* 81–100.

Herscher, E. (1989, November 27). AIDS child with two lesbian moms. *San Francisco Chronicle,* p. A8.

Hoeffer, B. (1981). Children's acquisition of sex-role behavior in lesbian-mother families. *American Journal of Orthopsychiatry, 51,* 536–544.

Hooker, E. (1969). Parental relations and male homosexuality in patient and nonpatient samples. *Journal of Consulting and Clinical Psychology, 33,* 140–142.

Howell, L. C., Weers, R., & Kleist, D. M. (1998). Counseling blended families. *The Family Journal, 6,* 42–45.

Humphreys, L. (1970). *Tea room trade.* Chicago: Aldine.

Isay, R. A. (1989). *Being homosexual: Gay men and their development.* New York: Farrar, Straus & Giroux.

Jay, K., & Young, A. (1979). *The gay report.* New York: Summit.

Jenny, C., Roesler, T., & Poyer, K. (1994). Are children at risk for sexual abuse by homosexuals? *Pediatrics, 94,* 41–44.

Johnson, W. (1992). Protestantism and gay and lesbian freedom. In B. Berzon (Ed.), *Positively gay: New approaches to gay and lesbian life* (pp. 142–155). Berkeley, CA: Celestial Arts.

Jones, B. M., & McFarlane, K. (1980). *Sexual abuse of children: Selected readings.* Washington, DC: National Center on Child Abuse and Neglect.

Jones, C. (1978). *Understanding gay relatives and friends.* New York: Seabury Press.

Kaufman, G., & Raphael, L. (1996). *Coming out of shame: Transforming gay and lesbian lives.* New York: Doubleday.

Kelley, H. (1967). Attribution theory in social psychology. In D. Levine (Ed.), *Nebraska Symposium on Motivation* (Vol. 15, pp. 97–123). Lincoln: University of Nebraska.

Kinsey, A., Pomeroy, W., & Martin, C. (1948). *Sexual behavior in the human male.* Philadelphia: Saunders.

Kirk, K., & Madsen, H. (1989). *After the ball: How America will conquer its fear and hatred of gays in the nineties.* New York: Doubleday.

Kirkpatrick, M., Smith, C., & Roy, R. (1981). Lesbian mothers and their children. *American Journal of Orthopsychiatry, 51,* 545–551.

Krier, B. (1988, November 7). America's becoming single-minded. *Charlotte Observer,* p. 6D.

Laird, J., & Green, R. J., (Eds.) (1996). *Lesbians and gays in couples and families: A handbook for therapists.* San Francisco: Jossey-Bass.

Lamb, M. E. (Ed.) (1981). *The role of the father in child development* (2nd ed.). New York: Wiley.

Lamb, M. E. (1986). *The father's role: Cross-cultural perspectives.* Hillsdale, NJ: Erlbaum.

Lamb, M. E. (1999). *Parenting and child development in "nontraditional" families.* Hillsdale, NJ: Erlbaum.

Lambda Legal Defense and Education Fund. (1997, August 28). Lesbian and gay parenting: A fact sheet [On-line]. Available: www.lambdalegal.org/documents/record?record1=31.

Lambda Legal Defense and Education Fund. (1998, July 30). North Carolina Supreme Court takes custody of sons from gay father [Press release, online]. Available: www.lambdalegal.org/documents/record?record1=278.

LaSala, M. (1998). Coupled gay men, parents, and in-laws: Intergeneration disapproval and the need for thick skin. *Families in Society, 76,* 585–595.

LeVay, S. (1991). A difference in hypothalamic structure between heterosexual and homosexual men. *Science,* pp. 1034–1037.

LeVay, S., & Hamer, D. (1994). Evidence for a biological influence in male homosexuality. *Science, 270,* 44–49.

Lewis, K. (1980). Children of lesbians: Their point of view. *Social Work, 25,* 200.

Logan, C. (1996). Homophobia? No! Homoprejudice. *Journal of Homosexuality, 31,* 31–53.

Maddox, B. (1982, February). Homosexual parents. *Psychology Today,* 62–69.

Mager, D. (1975). Faggot fathers. In K. Jay & A. Young (Eds.), *After you're out* (pp. 98–109). New York: Quick Fox.

Marciano, T. D. (1985). Homosexual marriage and parenthood should not be allowed. In H. Feldman & M. Feldman (Eds.), *Current controversies in marriage and family* (pp. 127–138). Thousand Oaks, CA: Sage.

Markowitz, L. (1999). Dangerous practice: Inside the conversion therapy controversy. *In the Family, 4*(3), 10–13.

Marmor, J. (1998). Homosexuality: Is etiology really important? *Journal of Gay and Lesbian Psychotherapy, 2*(4), 19–28.

Martin, A. (1993). *The lesbian and gay parenting handbook.* New York: HarperCollins.

McHenry, S., & Johnson, K. (1993). Homophobia in the therapist and gay or lesbian client: Conscious and unconscious conclusions in self-hate. *Psychotherapy, 30*(1), 341–348.

McIntyre, D. (1994). Gay parents and child custody: A struggle under the legal system. *Mediation Quarterly, 12*(2), 135–149.

McVinney, L. D. (1998). Social work practice with gay male couples. In G. P.

Mallon (Ed.), *Foundations of social work practice with lesbian and gay persons* (pp. 209–227). Binghamton, NY: Harrington Park Press.

Miller, B. (1978). Adult sexual resocialization: Adjustments toward stigmatized identity. *Alternate Lifestyles, 1,* 207–234.

Miller, B. (1979a). Gay fathers and their children. *Family Coordinator, 28,* 544–552.

Miller, B. (1979b). Unpromised paternity: The lifestyles of gay fathers. In M. Levine (Ed.), *Gay men: The sociology of male homosexuality* (pp. 239–252). New York: HarperCollins.

Montagu, A. (1978, August). A Kinsey report on homosexualities. *Psychology Today,* pp. 62–66.

Morin, S., & Schultz, S. (1978). The gay movement and the rights of children. *Journal of Social Issues, 34,* 137–148.

National Opinion Research Center (1985). *General social surveys, 1972–1985: Cumulative codebook.* Chicago: University of Chicago.

Newcomb, M. D. (1985). The role of relative parent personality in the development of heterosexuals, homosexuals, and transvestites. *Archives of Sexual Behavior, 14,* 147–164.

Nicolosi, J. (1991). *Reparative therapy of male homosexuality.* Northvale, NJ: Aronson.

Nugent, R. (1992). Catholicism: On the compatibility of sexuality and faith. In B. Berzon (Ed.), *Positively gay: New approaches to gay and lesbian life* (pp. 156–169). Berkeley, CA: Celestial Arts.

Patterson, C. J. (1992). Children of lesbian and gay parents. *Child Development, 63,* 1025–1042.

Patterson, C. J. (1994). Lesbian and gay families. *Current Directions in Psychological Science, 3,* 54–62.

Patterson, C. J., & Chan, R. W. (1996). Gay fathers. In M. E. Lamb (Ed.), *The role of the father in child development* (3rd ed., pp. 245–260). New York: Wiley.

Patterson, C. J., & Chan, R. W. (1999). Families headed by lesbian and gay parents. In M. E. Lamb (Ed.), *Parenting and child development in "nontraditional" families* (pp. 191–220). Hillsdale, NJ: Erlbaum.

Patterson, C. J., & Redding, R. E. (1996). Lesbian and gay families with children: Implications of social science research for policy. *Journal of Social Issues, 52,* 29–50.

Pennington, S. B. (1987). Children of lesbian mothers. In F. W. Bozett (Ed.), *Gay and lesbian parents* (pp. 58–74). New York: Praeger.

Perlstein, M. (1996). Integrating a gay, lesbian, or bisexual person's religious and spiritual needs and choices into psychotherapy. In C. Alexander (Ed.),

Gay and lesbian mental health: A sourcebook for practitioners (pp. 86–205). Binghamton, NY: Harrington Park Press.

Reider, N. (1948). The unmarried father. *American Journal of Orthopsychiatry, 18,* 230–237.

Richardson, D. (1981). Lesbian mothers. In J. Hart & D. Richardson (Eds.), *The theory and practice of homosexuality* (pp. 143–160). New York: Routledge.

Ricks, I. (1995, February 7). Fathers and son. *Advocate, 74,* 27–28.

Riddle, D. (1978). Relating to children: Gays as role models. *Journal of Social Issues, 34,* 38–58.

Riddle, D., & Arguelles, M. (1981). Children of gay parents: Homophobia's victims. In I. Stuart & L. Abt (Eds.), *Children of separation and divorce* (216–227). New York: Van Nostrand Reinhold.

Rivera, R. (1991). Sexual orientation and the law. In J. Gronsiorek & J. Weinrich (Eds.), *Homosexuality: Research implications for public policy* (pp. 81–100). Thousand Oaks, CA: Sage.

Robinson, B. E., & Barret, R. L. (1986). *The developing father: Emergent roles in contemporary society.* New York: Guilford Press.

Robinson, B. E., & Chase, N. (2000). *High-performing families: Causes, consequences, and clinical solutions.* Washington, DC: American Counseling Association.

Robinson, B. E., & Skeen, P. (1982). Sex-role orientation of gay fathers versus gay nonfathers. *Perceptual and Motor Skills, 55,* 1055–1059.

Robinson, B. E., Skeen, P., Flake-Hobson, C., & Herrman, M. (1982). Gay men's and women's perceptions of early family life and their relationships with parents. *Family Relations, 31,* 79–83.

Robinson, B. E., Skeen, P., & Walters, L. (1987, April). The AIDS epidemic hits home. *Psychology Today,* 48–52.

Robinson, B. E., Walters, L., & Skeen, P. (1989). Response of parents to learning that their child is homosexual and concern over AIDS: A national study. *Journal of Homosexuality, 18,* 59–80.

Ross, L. (1971). Mode of adjustment of married homosexuals. *Social Problems, 18,* 385–393.

Ross, M. (1983). *The married homosexual man.* New York: Routledge.

Rudolph, J. (1988). Counselor attitudes toward homosexuality: A review of the literature. *Journal of Counseling and Development, 67,* 165–168.

Saffron, L. (1996). *What about the children? Sons and daughters of lesbians and gay parents talk about their lives.* London: Cassell.

Scallen, R. (1981). An investigation of paternal attitudes and behaviors in homosexual and heterosexual fathers. (Doctoral dissertation, California School of Professional Psychology). *Dissertation Abstracts International, 42,* 3809B.

Schulenburg, J. (1985). *Gay parenting: A complete guide for gay men and lesbians with children.* New York: Doubleday.

Seow, C. L. (1996). *Homosexuality and the Christian community.* Louisville, KY: Westminster John Knox Press.

Shordone, A. J. (1993). *Gay men choosing fatherhood.* Unpublished doctoral dissertation, City University of New York.

Skeen, P., & Robinson, B. E. (1984). Family backgrounds of gay fathers: A descriptive study. *Psychological Reports, 54,* 999–1005.

Skeen, P., & Robinson, B. E. (1985). Gay fathers' and gay nonfathers' relationship with their parents. *Journal of Sex Research, 21,* 86–91.

Skeen, P., Walters, L., & Robinson, B. E. (1988). How parents of gays react to their children's homosexuality and to the threat of AIDS. *Journal of Psychosocial Nursing, 26,* 7–10.

Spada, J. (1979). *The Spada report.* New York: New American Library.

Steckel, A. (1987). Psychosocial development of children of lesbian mothers. In F. W. Bozett (Ed.), *Gay and lesbian parents* (pp. 203–221). New York: Praeger.

Storms, M. (1978). Attitudes towards homosexuality and femininity in men. *Journal of Homosexuality, 3,* 257–266.

Storms, M. (1980). Theories of sexual orientation. *Journal of Personality and Social Psychology, 38,* 783–792.

Stradler, S. (1993, August). *Non-custodial gay fathers.* Paper presented at the annual meeting of the American Psychological Association, Toronto.

Strommen, E. (1989). "You're a what?": Family member reactions to the disclosure of homosexuality. *Journal of Homosexuality, 18,* 37–58.

Tasker, F. L., & Golombok, S. (1997). *Growing up in a lesbian family.* New York: Guilford Press.

Thompson, B. (1986, May). *Two reasons why multivariate methods are usually vital.* Paper presented at the Mid-South Educational Research Association, Memphis, TN.

Turner, P. H., Scadden, L., & Harris, M. B. (1990). Parenting in gay and lesbian families. *Journal of Gay and Lesbian Psychotherapy, 1*(3), 55–66.

Visher, E. B., & Visher, J. S. (1978). Common problems of stepparents and their spouses. *American Journal of Orthopsychiatry, 48,* 252–262.

Voeller, B., & Walters, J. (1978). Gay fathers. *Family Coordinator, 27,* 149–157.

Walters, L. H., & Elam, A. W. (1985). The father and the law. *American Behavioral Scientist, 29,* 78–111.

Warren, C. (1980). Homosexuality and stigma. In J. Marmor (Ed.), *Homosexual behavior* (pp. 123–141). New York: Basic Books.

Weeks, R., Derdeyn, A., & Langman, M. (1975). Two cases of children of homosexuals. *Child Psychiatry and Human Development*, 6, 26–32.

Weinberg, G. (1972). *Society and the healthy homosexual*. New York: Doubleday.

White, M. (1994). *Stranger at the gate: To be gay and Christian in America*. New York: Simon & Schuster.

Whitehead, S. L. (1997). *The truth shall set you free: A memoir of a family's passage from fundamentalism to a new understanding of faith, love, and sexual identity*. San Francisco: Harper.

Woodman, H. J., & Lenna, H. R. (1980). *Counseling with gay men and women: A guide for facilitating positive life styles*. San Francisco: Jossey-Bass.

Wyers, N. L. (1987). Lesbian and gay spouses and parents: Homosexuality in the family. *Social Work*, 32, 143–148.

Zugar, B. (1980). Homosexuality and parental guilt. *British Journal of Psychiatry*, 137, 55–57.

The Authors

Bob Barret, Ph.D., is professor of counseling at the University of North Carolina at Charlotte. As a psychologist, he has been in private practice for twenty years. He is also a gay father and a grandfather of five. Barret's current writings include *Counseling Gay Men and Lesbians*, coauthored with Colleen Logan, and *Ethical Issues in HIV-Related Psychotherapy* with Jon Anderson. He has also written about gay spirituality and has been active in helping the mental health professions understand the dangers of so-called reparative and conversion therapies. An advocate for increased understanding of all sexual minorities, Barret has written for several newspapers across the country.

Bryan E. Robinson, Ph.D., is professor of counseling, special education, and child development at the University of North Carolina at Charlotte. He maintains a private psychotherapy practice in Charlotte and writes a monthly column for *Your Health* magazine. He has authored over twenty-five books and more than one hundred research publications on family issues, particularly as they affect gay men and lesbians. In 1998, Robinson received the Extended Research Award from the American Counseling Association for his research. His most recent books are *Chained to the Desk: A Guidebook for Workaholics, Their Partners and Children and the Clinicians Who Treat Them* (NYU Press, 1998) and *Don't Let Your Mind Stunt Your Growth* (New Harbinger Publications, 2000).

Index